The Agent Playbook

Essential Strategies for Success in Real Estate

Jessica Souza

Copyright © 2024 by Jessica Souza

All rights reserved.

No portion of this book may be reproduced in any form without written permission from the publisher or author, except as permitted by U.S. copyright law.

Table of Contents

Introduction 1

1: Finding Your Brokerage Soulmate 15

2: Assembling Your Real Estate Dream Team 33

3: Your Business Blueprints 49

4: Mastering Commissions & Cash Flow 65

5: Navigating Real Estate Taxes & Laws 83

6: Finding Your Ideal Client 99

7: Creating a Brand That Connects 113

8: Operating with Excellence 129

9: Building a Support Network 147

Epilogue 159

Acknowledgements 163

Appendix I 165

Appendix II 171

Suggested Further Reading 173

About the Author 175

For My Girls

May you courageously leap towards your dreams.

Anything is possible with passion, perseverance, and heart.

> Push through where others might step back.

Introduction

Welcome to the exciting first step of your promising new career! Yes, stepping into the real estate world is like opening the door to a room filled with opportunities—it's exhilarating, a bit daunting, but oh so rewarding. But let's get real—passing the real estate exam is far from a walk in the park. With a national average pass rate hovering around 46%, the state exam isn't a test that everyone just breezes through. But you? You're not just anyone. You've got the grit and the drive to push through where others might step back.

My own journey in real estate is a bit unconventional. Prior to ever actually entering the field, I worked in a variety of industries—seven years in higher education, seven years as a professional photographer, and eight years as a field market manager at a marketing firm for a variety of brands like Dell, Microsoft, Absolut, and Jeep. A diverse resume, I know. But, through each of my roles I was able to master a variety of different skills—from systems and processes to marketing and sales.

My first year as a college recruiter I increased admission by over 400% for our Venice, Florida, campus. This got the attention of our other campus recruiters and led to adoption of my strategies college-wide. As a professional photographer, beyond photographing sweet newborn babies, I had the pleasure of mentoring and coaching hundreds of photographers nationwide in business operations. Much like real estate agents, photographers often struggle to look at themselves as business owners. Empowering them in their businesses became a huge passion of mine and continues to fuel me as I do the same for real estate agents.

My years as a field market manager were filled with training ambassadors on program objectives, understanding brand messaging, crafting memorable customer experiences, understanding KPIs (key performance indicators), and being able to deliver continued business growth in our target market. Basically, I was in a sales associate bootcamp and just didn't know it.

In 2018, I started as an operations director under a high-producing real estate team at a corporate real estate brokerage. I was able to apply my diverse skillset to the real estate industry and fell in love! A few months after joining the team, I decided to get my license. However, once I was licensed, I quickly realized we needed a brokerage change—the support, fees, and culture just weren't a good fit. Though it took some convincing, eventually the whole team decided to move to an independent brokerage and embraced everything the brokerage stood for.

However, I eventually outgrew my role within the team and decided to shift my focus to new construction. After being in new construction for two years—*plot twist!*—I went back to that amazing independent brokerage (told you I loved it!), snagged my broker's license, and made partner. Now, I have the pleasure of overseeing more than 120 agents and interviewing dozens more each year. With this, I've gotten to see firsthand what makes or breaks new agents and hear about what missteps seasoned pros made in their journey. This fueled my passion to share my knowledge with those stepping into the world of real estate for the first time and provide the guidance needed to ease the wild transition into the field.

I love this industry—I'm all about helping people own their dream home. But where I truly shine? Agent development and business growth. That's my jam. Many new agents enter the field thinking they're ready to conquer the world. The licensing courses are great for passing the test—trust me, you'll know exactly how many square feet are in an acre and enough acronyms to write a dictionary. But here's the kicker: those courses don't teach you how to *be* a real estate agent. They don't cover the day-to-day grind, how to juggle clients, market properties, or seal deals. As a result, so many new agents struggle, and it has nothing to do with a lack of desire to succeed.

That's exactly why I wrote *The Agent Playbook*. Think of it as your unofficial guide to building a flourishing real estate career. We're going beyond the basics. From finding the right brokerage to streamlining daily tasks—we've got a lot of ground to cover!

GETTING STARTED

Beginning your journey in your real estate career starts with a solid foundation, quite literally laying the groundwork for all your future successes. But before you can dazzle clients with your house matchmaking skills, you need to be licensed. This process is your first step towards becoming a real estate sales associate. However, there are really two main pieces to getting started —getting licensed and choosing the right brokerage. Without a brokerage you cannot sell, even with your sales associate license.

Choosing the right real estate course is one of the first significant decisions you'll make. This choice can set the tone for your learning experience and ultimately influence how well-prepared you feel to tackle the state exam. You want to select a course format that best suits not only your schedule, but your learning style. Many choose an online option because of the flexibility in the course schedule. However, I've seen a lot of agents that chose online learning but do not retain information well in that setting. Most online courses are self-paced and not live or even recorded video content. You're left to read the curriculum—yes, all of it. As I'm sure you can imagine, retaining or even simply understanding everything you read can be a challenge—which is why many end up having to reinvest time and money into an in-person course in order to actually pass the state exam.

Nobody knows you better than yourself, so be mindful when making your course selection. Cost is not always a direct success indicator. More expensive doesn't always mean better. Look at online reviews, instructor expertise, learning resources, student support, and additional services being offered, like exam prep and tutoring.

Choosing the right real estate course is more than just a prerequisite for getting licensed—it's an investment in your future success in the industry. Take the time to carefully evaluate your options, considering how each course aligns with your learning style, professional goals, and personal commitments. The right course will not only prepare you for the exam, but will also lay a solid foundation for a successful career in real estate.

Once you complete the real estate course and receive your approval to test, the state exam is your gateway to your real estate license. Passing this exam proves that you have not only the foundational knowledge necessary for a real estate career, but also the ability to apply what you've learned. Set yourself up for success by joining study groups, utilizing practice exams, and if necessary, enrolling in additional prep courses to boost your confidence. *You've got this!*

Once you've passed your exam and are officially a licensed real estate agent, the next immediate step is to align yourself with a brokerage. Nothing boosts your ego like beginning the process of getting your license. While the curriculum and test aren't easy, once you've enrolled in a real estate course, your phone, email, and mailbox will be flooded with recruiters from real estate brokerages looking to snap you up! It can be very exciting to have so many people interested in having you on their team. But this is one of the biggest decisions of your career—so do. not. rush. it. In fact, this is so important I've dedicated all of Chapter 1 specifically to finding your brokerage soulmate!

UNDERSTANDING THE LINGO

Before we dive deeper into the nuts and bolts of real estate, let's take a moment to untangle some terms that often trip up newcomers. You've probably heard the terms "real estate agent" and "Realtor" used interchangeably, right? Well, they're similar, but not the same—kind of like all squares are rectangles, but not all rectangles are squares.

Here's the deal: every Realtor is a real estate agent, but not every real estate agent is a Realtor. Confused yet? Hang tight! The term "Realtor" is actually a registered trademark. It refers to a real estate agent who is a member of the National Association of Realtors (NAR), which is the largest trade association in the U.S.

NAR isn't just about paying dues and getting a membership card. It's about committing to a code of ethics that emphasizes professionalism, client interests, and community involvement. This code isn't just a bunch of rules—it's a declaration of commitment to practice real estate with the highest standards of integrity and honesty. By adhering to these standards, Realtors pledge to treat all parties fairly and maintain their clients' trust, making them stand out in the industry.

Being a Realtor can give you a leg up in several ways:
- **Trust and Credibility:** Clients often feel more secure knowing they're working with someone who's pledged

to uphold the NAR's strong ethical standards. This can be a huge advantage in building relationships and growing your business.

- **Resources and Support:** Realtors have access to a wide array of professional tools, market data, and continuing education programs provided by the NAR. These resources can be invaluable in keeping you informed and ahead of the curve.
- **Networking Opportunities:** The NAR hosts events, conferences, and seminars that bring real estate professionals together from across the country. These gatherings are golden opportunities for networking, learning from seasoned pros, and staying updated on industry trends.

Deciding whether to become a Realtor hinges on your career aspirations, ethical values, and specific business needs. At first glance, the difference might not seem substantial, but the benefits of affiliating with a respected organization like the National Association of Realtors can impact your professional image. It's important to consider this decision carefully, especially since some brokerages might require membership.

THE OPPORTUNITIES ARE ENDLESS

Real estate has so many different opportunities, each tailored to match your personal style and career aspirations. This isn't a one-path journey. Real estate is a huge industry that you can explore based on what excites you most.

Whether you're drawn to the charm of residential homes or the buzz of commercial real estate, the industry molds to fit you perfectly, not the other way around.

If residential properties are your calling, you're in for a treat. Residential real estate is as varied as the people you'll meet. Dive into luxury real estate if you have an eye for elegant homes and a network that desires the finer things. Or maybe you find joy in helping first-time homebuyers navigate their biggest purchase; the gratitude and lasting relationships can be incredibly rewarding. Interested in something a bit quirky or unique? Specialize in historic or eco-friendly homes. The residential market has a place for everyone.

On the flip side, commercial real estate has a whole new level of dynamics. It's about more than just buildings; it's about understanding market economics, long-term investment strategies, and the intricate needs of businesses. Whether it's retail spaces, office buildings, or multi-unit residential complexes, commercial real estate demands insight into market trends and business needs. It can be more complex but also potentially more lucrative, with higher stakes and bigger deals.

Don't forget about land sales, industrial properties, or even agricultural real estate. Each of these areas offers unique challenges and rewards and requires specific knowledge. Specializing in vacant land, for example, might involve selling undeveloped land slated for development, requiring skills in zoning laws, environmental regulations, and development potential. Industrial real estate, meanwhile, could have you dealing with warehouses or manufacturing facilities, where logistics and location are the focus.

Diversifying your real estate knowledge isn't just about keeping things interesting—it's about resilience. The more areas you understand and can operate in, the more you can adapt to market shifts and economic changes. This diversification also enables you to serve a broader range of clients, enhancing your business stability and growth potential.

What makes the real estate industry so special is that you get to design your career around your strengths, passions, and lifestyle goals. Whether it's helping families find their first home, assisting corporations in locating the perfect business space, or selling luxurious estates, your real estate career can be whatever you want it to be. This flexibility to specialize or generalize as you grow allows you to continuously shape your path, ensuring that your career never feels stagnant.

Real estate is a field where your career doesn't just grow; it evolves alongside you. In your journey, you'll likely meet what I call "real estate OGs" (original gangsters)—seasoned pros who could have retired long ago but remain driven by a deep passion for the industry. The opportunities here are boundless, offering a rewarding and dynamic career path that's as thrilling on your first day as it is decades later. Whether you're sketching out open houses on weekends or sealing deals in high-rise buildings, real estate provides a canvas as vast as your ambitions.

But it isn't all sunshine and rainbows. Let's talk about the challenges. The market will fluctuate, sometimes unpredictably. Some months you'll feel on top of the world, and others, you might wonder if you forgot to pay your phone bill because your phone isn't ringing. Early on, building a client base will test your networking savvy and marketing skills. The paperwork can be overwhelming at times, from disclosures to contracts. But here's the deal—these hurdles are stepping stones to your growth and success. With each challenge, you'll gain invaluable skills that will only make you sharper, more intuitive, and better equipped.

SETTING THE RIGHT EXPECTATIONS

Embarking on a career in real estate isn't a sprint; think of it more like a marathon with scenic stops. It's a journey filled with learning curves, occasional setbacks, and many victories. Success in this field doesn't happen overnight, and that's perfectly okay. In fact, many do not see their first commission check for six months *(I know—that wasn't in your pre-licensing curriculum)*. It's important to set realistic, achievable goals from the start and give yourself the space and grace to learn and grow.

Real estate is a field where patience truly pays off. The early days might involve a lot of groundwork—networking, learning the local market, understanding client needs, and mastering the art of negotiation. These are your building blocks for a successful career. With hard work, dedication, and a bit of patience, the results will surely come.

Imagine the thrill of closing your first big deal, the joy of seeing a family move into their dream home, or the satisfaction when an investor thanks you for finding the perfect property. These moments are not just rewarding—they're affirmations that you're making a real impact. Each successful transaction builds your reputation and opens doors to new opportunities. It is so much more than just a sales job. We are advising people through some of the biggest transactions of their lives. That experience is something they will never forget, and you get to be part of that story.

Starting off on the right foot in real estate means arming yourself with knowledge, and what better way to do that than investing in this book? Consider this part of your essential toolkit for success in real estate. It's designed to help you navigate through the complexities of getting started in real estate with ease.

The Agent Playbook is more than just a collection of information; it's a treasure trove of actionable insights and practical advice I have compiled over years of working with agents—new and seasoned. The gap between licensed and professional is substantial, which is why I designed this book to help you sidestep common pitfalls and seize opportunities right from the start. By investing in your education, you're not just reading—you're equipping yourself with the knowledge and confidence needed to excel in your new career.

As you progress, treat every experience as a learning opportunity. Whether you're navigating challenging negotiations, experimenting with new marketing strategies, or managing difficult clients, each situation is a chance to sharpen your skills—even when it gets frustrating (and yes, it can be really frustrating!). Embrace these moments, reflect on them, and continuously seek ways to improve.

Setting the right expectations for your real estate career means recognizing that while the road might be long and occasionally bumpy, it is also lined with chances to grow professionally and personally. With this book in hand, you're preparing to conquer the world of real estate, one property at a time. So buckle up and get ready for an exciting ride into your future career, filled with achievements and real impact.

Embrace the journey
of learning
and achieving.

1

Finding Your Brokerage Soulmate

A Guide to Finding the Right Brokerage

Finding the right brokerage is a lot like dating—you're looking for that special someone who not only gets you, but also brings out your best. It's about finding a place that feels like home, where you're supported, understood, and given the room to flourish. Think of it as seeking your brokerage soulmate, the kind that not only vibes with your style, but also challenges you to stretch and grow.

In my conversations with agents interested in joining our brokerage, a common theme emerges: many wish they had taken the time to interview more options before committing to their first brokerage. However, when you're freshly licensed or even studying for your exam, recruiters swarm, trying to get you to commit to joining their team. While it can be extremely flattering to have all of these brokerages interested in you, a quick commitment can lead to missed connections with brokerages that might be a better fit.

The reality is, with so many brokerage models out there, the support and expectations vary widely. It's crucial to take your time and really understand what each brokerage offers, ensuring their approach aligns with your own professional needs and goals.

Let's dive into the essentials of picking a brokerage that feels like a perfect match, one where you can thrive and achieve your fullest potential in the real estate world.

Before you start swiping right on every brokerage that pops up, take a moment to truly understand what you need. Just like in dating, knowing what you're looking for is the first step to finding a match that lights up your world. Are you craving extensive training programs that guide you through every twist and turn? Perhaps you're seeking a strong mentorship culture where seasoned pros are eager to pass the baton and cheer you on from the sidelines. Or maybe you're a tech whiz looking for cutting-edge technology and innovative marketing tools that can catapult your listings into the spotlight.

Think about what your day-to-day looks like and what's going to make it not just manageable, but enjoyable. Do you thrive in a bustling, energetic office environment, or do you prefer a sleek, digital-first approach that lets you work seamlessly from anywhere?

Despite how it may seem, the brokerages aren't just interviewing you—you are also interviewing the brokerages.

That's why identifying your non-negotiables is so important. It sets you up for success in an environment that feels custom-made for you. These are the must-haves that will not only support your growth, but also fuel your passion and keep you engaged in your real estate journey. With these priorities in mind, you can easily make your way through all of your available options with confidence and clarity, ensuring that when you do make a match, it's with a brokerage that truly complements your ambitions and amplifies your strengths.

CULTURE AND VALUES

Just like in any relationship, shared values are the heart and soul of your connection with a brokerage. When you're exploring potential homes for your career, really dive into the culture. What's the energy like when you walk through the door? Is it a competitive sprint or a collaborative marathon? Are people smiling and engaged, or does it feel like every agent for themselves?

It's important to remember that a brokerage's corporate culture might not always match the local office vibe. I've experienced this firsthand with a large corporate brokerage that boasted an amazing culture, but the reality at the local level was quite different. It was sold to me as a collaborative and encouraging environment—but once I was amongst the other agents in the office, the vibe was quite the opposite.

Honestly, the best folks to chat with are the current and past agents at the specific office you're considering. You'll want to personally select agents at random to chat with—

don't rely on the names provided to you from the brokerage. Their insights on daily interactions, office dynamics, and the managing broker's style are invaluable.

How does the brokerage celebrate achievements? Is it in a way that resonates with you? Perhaps you'd love your sales volume shared on the brokerage's social media, or maybe you prefer quieter, more personal acknowledgments. Does the brokerage support and invest in continuous learning and professional development without extra costs? You want to feel electric every time you step into the office, part of an environment that not only drives you to achieve your goals, but celebrates every victory along the way.

Ultimately, you want a brokerage that acts as a cheerleader for your career—supporting you through the highs and lows and inspiring you to constantly reach for more. It's about finding a professional family where the values align so closely with your own that every day propels you towards something greater. Remember, the right brokerage doesn't just fit your career—it elevates it.

SUPPORT AND TRAINING

A top-tier brokerage isn't just about the flashy perks; it offers a robust suite of support systems designed to navigate you through the twists and turns of your real estate journey. I've heard countless stories about brokers who are simply non-existent and never available when you need them most. This might work for seasoned agents, but most need a broker who is engaged, responsive, and eager to assist.

Imagine having a stellar team behind you so you can focus on what you do best—connecting with clients, closing deals, and scouting new opportunities. This kind of support is about more than just convenience; it's about freeing you to create those happy client stories we all aim for. Some brokerages offer in-house transaction coordinators to manage all paperwork from start to finish, while others might only review documents for compliance. Take a moment to think about what you want your career to look like and the role you expect your brokerage to play.

Then there's the training—*oh, the training!* It's crucial, especially for new agents. Your pre-licensing course might have helped you pass the exam, but being a successful agent is about so much more than just getting licensed. A brokerage that values learning and development will provide regular workshops, webinars, and training sessions to help you manage day-to-day tasks and navigate your first contracts. But remember, not all training is created equal. Are these sessions in-person or online? Do they cost extra? How often are they held? Is personalized coaching available to help you tackle specific challenges?

COMPETE VS. NON-COMPETE BROKER

Deciding between working for a broker who's out there closing deals or one who's more like a behind-the-scenes guru guiding your career can feel a bit like choosing between a bustling city vibe and a supportive small-town community. Both have their perks and quirks.

WORKING FOR A BROKER WHO ALSO SELLS

PROS

1. Real-Time Learning: It's like having a front-row seat at a blockbuster—watch and learn from a pro who's still swinging in the real estate arena.

2. Networking Gold: Tag along with a power player. A broker who's active in the market can introduce you to influential people and opportunities that might otherwise be out of reach.

3. Vibrant Energy: There's a certain buzz you get from working in a team where everyone's hustling. It's inspiring, contagious, and can seriously motivate you to up your own game.

CONS

1. Competition for Leads: It can sometimes feel like you're sharing a stage with a seasoned star. This might mean fewer chances to shine if your broker is also chasing the spotlight.

2. Divided Attention: Ever needed advice but got the "I'm slammed" response? When your broker is also closing deals, you might not always get the support or time you need right when you need it.

3. Potential for Conflict: Things can get tricky if there's a clash between what's best for you and what's best for your broker's own deals.

WORKING FOR A NON-COMPETE BROKER

PROS

1. Dedicated Support: It's like having a mentor who's all about boosting your career. This kind of broker offers endless support, tools, and resources to help you grow.

2. Fairer Lead Distribution: The leads are spread more evenly when your broker isn't competing with you. This means more opportunities to develop your own client relationships.

3. Customized Growth: They're focused on your success and often provide personalized training and development programs to help you find your niche and excel in it.

CONS

1. Less On-the-Ground Insight: Without the daily sales grind, you might miss out on those gritty, real-world experiences that teach so much about the hustle of real estate.

2. Quieter Office Atmosphere: If you thrive on high energy and constant movement, a more subdued office focusing on support rather than sales might not buzz enough for you.

3. Reliance on Provided Leads: There's a comfort in having leads handed to you, but it might make you a bit too cozy. Learning to generate your own leads is crucial for long-term success.

Choosing the right broker is about matching their style with your career aspirations. Are you looking for a mentor who will nurture your growth, or do you want to jump into the high-energy world of a top seller? Each has its magic, so pick the path that lights up your real estate journey the brightest!

TECHNOLOGY AND TOOLS

Let's talk tech. Today, being tech-savvy is non-negotiable. The right brokerage equips you with cutting-edge tools to streamline your processes, boost your marketing, and manage client relationships effortlessly. From CRM (Customer Relationship Management) systems that track every detail to analytics platforms that predict market trends, these tools are more than just nice-to-have; they're a must.

However, it's easy to get distracted by the latest gadgets. Technology should enhance, not overshadow, your core needs, like broker support and training. I've spoken with many agents who don't even use the fantastic tools provided by their brokerages because, while the tech is impressive, the training and implementation support are lacking.

Having solid tools is a no-brainer—like electronic signing capabilities and a way to manage your client communications. But there is a balance between tech offerings and cost. Whether you choose to invest in your own tech solutions or use what's provided, make sure you understand how to integrate these tools into your everyday work effectively.

MARKET PRESENCE AND REPUTATION

In real estate, reputation really is everything. It's the golden ticket that can open doors, forge connections, and set the stage for your success. When you're choosing where to hang your hat (and your license!), diving into the brokerage's reputation isn't just smart—it's essential.

Start by digging into their standing within the industry. What's the buzz? Are they known for integrity and excellence, or do whispers of dissatisfaction follow them around? How do they stack up in market presence? Are their signs on every corner, or do they take a more boutique approach? Each tells a story of success in its own unique way.

But here's the real tea: How well do they hold up when the market swings? Real estate is as much about weathering storms as it is about basking in sunshine. A brokerage with a robust track record isn't just surviving in both booming and slow markets; they're thriving. They adapt, innovate, and pivot their strategies to ensure that no matter the economic climate, they come out on top.

Recently, when most brokerages were closing office locations or downsizing, we chose to double down and invest in our agents, opening a new location in one of the fastest-growing communities in the nation. This commitment to our agents is one of the many things that I believe sets us apart in our market.

Additionally, a truly remarkable brokerage is deeply embedded in the community. They're not just present during transactions; they're part of the local fabric, participating in community events, supporting local charities, and contributing to the area's growth and well-being. This level of community involvement not only enhances their reputation, but also enriches your network and connects you more deeply with potential clients who value local commitment. When you're at the local youth soccer field, is the brokerage you're considering listed as a business sponsor? What about at your local chamber of commerce or the county schools? For some agents this may be less important. But from my experience, brokerages that play an integral role in the community also tend to have the respect of their neighbors, which, in turn, benefits their business significantly.

Choosing a brokerage with a stellar reputation, proven track record, and strong community ties is like choosing a mentor who can't wait to see you shine. It's about more than just a name; it's about joining a legacy of excellence that elevates your own aspirations. Here, you're not just joining a team; you're becoming part of a story—a story of success, resilience, relentless pursuit of greatness, and genuine community engagement. Let's make sure it's a story worth telling.

FINANCIAL STRUCTURE AND FEES

Dive into the nitty-gritty of financials with a potential brokerage. How transparent are they about commissions, fees, and other financial details? Brokerage structures can vary—some may offer simple commission splits, while others might have tiered systems based on performance, along with various fees like transaction fees, monthly dues, and annual caps. If

THE AGENT PLAYBOOK

this world of numbers sounds dizzying, ask to walk through a hypothetical sale during your interview to see how much you'd actually take home after all the deductions. For instance, imagine you sell a single-family home for $200,000. Ask about every possible fee—office, admin, marketing, printing, tech, transaction, corporate fees, and your commission split. What would your net be?

EXAMPLE BROKERAGE FEE COMPARISON CHART:

Brokerage Name	Brokerage A	Brokerage B	Brokerage C
Commission Split	70/30	80/20	100%
Franchise Fee	$5,000/Year	No Fee	$5,000/Year
Desk Fees	$100/Month	No Fee	$1,200/Month
Transaction Fees	$400/Closing	No Fee	$350/Closing
E & O Fees	No Fee	No Fee	No Fee
Other Fees (e.g., Tech, Marketing)	$50/Month Tech + $30/Month Marketing	$50/Month Tech	$200 Tech Fee
Annual Caps	$20,000	No Cap	No Cap

Get your brokerage comparison worksheet at:
WWW.JESSICA-SOUZA.COM/MORE

Choosing a brokerage isn't just about who offers you the most money at the end of the day. It's about whose offer aligns best with your needs and goals and taking the time to understand the full package, ensuring there are no surprises with hidden fees. A brokerage that's upfront about these things builds a relationship based on trust—crucial for your peace of mind and professional growth.

    When interviewing with potential brokerages, having a set of well-thought-out questions can help you gauge whether the brokerage aligns with your career goals and values. Here's a comprehensive list of interview questions that a real estate agent might consider asking during their brokerage interviews:

CULTURE AND VALUES:

- Can you describe the culture here at the brokerage?
- What are your core values?
- How do you support collaboration among agents?
- How frequently do you review agent performance, and what does that process look like?
- What kind of feedback can I expect to receive, and who will it come from?

SUPPORT AND TRAINING:

- What kinds of administrative support do agents receive here?

- Can you tell me about the training and development programs available? Are they included in the brokerage fees?
- How accessible are the brokers or mentors when I need guidance?
- What opportunities are there for professional growth and advancement within the brokerage?
- How does the brokerage support agents looking to expand into new market areas or specialties?
- What are the average sales figures for new agents in their first year here?
- How does the brokerage measure success and support agents in meeting their targets?

TECHNOLOGY AND TOOLS:

- What technology and marketing tools does the brokerage provide?
- Are there additional costs for accessing these tools?
- Is there a review process for marketing collateral or guidelines that need to be followed?
- How does the brokerage ensure that agents are proficient in using these tools?

MARKET PRESENCE AND REPUTATION:

- How does the brokerage maintain its reputation in the market?

- What strategies are in place to thrive in both booming and slow markets?
- How does the brokerage handle advertising and promotions for agents and listings?
- Can you provide examples of how the brokerage is involved in the local community?
- Are agents encouraged to participate in community events?

FINANCIAL STRUCTURE AND FEES:
- What is the commission structure?
- Do you provide leads? If so, is there a change in the commission split?
- Are there any desk fees, transaction fees, or other charges that I should be aware of?
- Could you walk me through a typical transaction and how fees are applied?

Last but not least, always trust your instincts. After you've crunched the numbers, visited offices, and chatted with potential teammates, your gut feeling about a brokerage might just be the most telling sign of all. Ask yourself: Do you feel welcomed and valued here? Is there a sense of community? Does it feel like a place where you can truly belong and thrive? If there's even a whisper of doubt, it might be a sign to keep looking. You deserve a brokerage that feels like home, one where you're not just another agent, but a valued member of a supportive family.

Finding your brokerage soulmate is more about heart than contracts. It's not about jumping at the first opportunity or the one with the best financial incentives. It's about finding that perfect fit, a place that sparks your passion and propels your career forward at warp speed. Take your time, do your homework, and really listen to how you feel when you walk through the doors of what could be your new professional home.

Just like the most enduring relationships, the right brokerage should inspire confidence and excitement in you—it should make you feel like you can conquer the world, or at least make a significant mark on the real estate market in your area. Remember, this isn't just a business decision; it's a choice about where you will grow, flourish, and build your dreams. So, tune in to your inner voice—it's your ultimate guide in this journey.

Commit to the highest standards of your profession.

2

Assembling Your Real Estate Dream Team

The Art of Finding the Right Partners

The phrase "it takes a village" couldn't be more applicable than in building your real estate career. Think of yourself as the quarterback of your own real estate game. Like any standout sports hero, you need a powerhouse team behind you to secure those victories. We're not just filling roles here; we're assembling a team of A-players who bring their best to every game. This means finding a real estate mentor to guide you, a savvy CPA to manage your finances with finesse, and perhaps even a creative photographer whose stunning shots make your listings stand out.

In this chapter, we'll explore how to build a dream team that not only complements your strengths, but also balances your weaknesses. After all, you want to be out there making magic happen—negotiating deals, wowing clients, and closing sales—not sweating the small stuff.

Here's the game plan:

CRAFTING YOUR DREAM TEAM

Before you start scouting, let's get crystal clear about what your dream really looks like. What are your big, bold goals? Whether you aim to dominate the downtown luxury market or become the go-to guru for first-time homebuyers, understanding your goals will help you determine who you need by your side.

Reflect on your day-to-day operations. What comes easily to you? Perhaps it's networking, or maybe it is negotiating the best terms for your clients. Recognizing your strengths not only boosts your confidence, but also highlights where you excel.

Now, consider where you're less confident. Does the thought of sorting through paperwork make you cringe, or do the complexities of digital marketing strategies seem overwhelming? These are your cues for support. It's easy, especially early on, to think you need to do everything yourself or to undervalue your time, spending hours on tasks that a professional could handle more efficiently and economically.

It's perfectly okay not to be a jack-of-all-trades. In fact, acknowledging where you need help is the first critical step toward building a team that complements your abilities and fills in the gaps. This isn't just about filling roles—it's about creating a synergistic environment where each team member's strengths are utilized and their weaknesses are supported. By deeply understanding your own needs, you set the stage for bringing in people who not only meet these needs, but also elevate your business.

So, take a moment to jot down your top goals for the next year, the tasks you excel at, and the areas where you could use some help. This exercise isn't just about understanding your business—it's about understanding yourself. From this self-awareness comes the clarity that will guide your decisions as you handpick each member of your dream team.

Remember, every great team starts with a great leader—knowing what you need is the first step in becoming the leader your team will rally behind. Let's turn those dreams into reality by being intentional about who we bring on board!

After analyzing hundreds of successful agents and their support systems, I've compiled a comprehensive list of roles you may consider to kickstart your team-building. Remember, you likely won't need to fill all these roles immediately, but keep them in mind as your business grows. You'll see that the list is separated into two sections, Must-Haves and Future Needs. But this list is fluid—move vendors around to the section that makes sense to you. After all, this is your business!

MUST-HAVES:

- **Banker:** A small business banking contact from your local bank. You're more than just a real estate agent, you're a small business owner—an entrepreneur! Having a contact at your local bank that focuses on small business banking will prove to be an asset as you set up your business accounts and make strategic decisions as your business grows.

- **CPA/Accountant:** Someone to manage your business finances and navigate tax complexities. If all you've known is being a W2 employee, switching to business ownership can be a rude awakening come tax time. Tax professionals are here to help guide you in everything from business formation to maximizing tax write-offs.

- **Print Shop:** Agents are extremely creative when it comes to marketing strategies, and that includes physical marketing materials like yard signs, business cards, and branded merchandise. Having a local print shop that produces high-quality products with quick turnaround times is essential to remaining top of mind in your community.

- **Real Estate Photographer/Videographer:** A creator of compelling visual content for your listings. If you don't know already, most buyers start their home search online, which means your listing needs to stand out online. A good photographer/videographer is going to make sure your listing is shown at its best and will set it apart from the competition who wanted to save the money and take poorly lit photos with their phone. They also know your local MLS photo/video requirements and restrictions so you don't get fined for non-compliance.

- **Portrait Photographer:** Not all photographers are the same. Your real estate photographer may know all the angles to really show off your listing's features, but absolutely butcher a professional headshot. Having a photographer that is going to make you look and feel good and can capture professional headshots and branding/marketing photos for social media and print ads is a must! Whether or not you want it to be true, your face is your brand in this industry, and having up-to-date, quality headshots makes a difference.

- **Graphic Designer:** Designs personal branding materials and advertisements—and you're going to need a lot of advertisements! From just-listed and just-sold postcards, to that ad in your local paper—there are so many needs for a professional who can whip together an eye-catching graphic and who knows the proper resolution, bleeds, margins, color profile, file type, font size, etc. Even if they simply create some templates that you can work from, the initial setup of these designs will save you hours on Canva (a web-based graphic design tool) and have the punch you need to make a good impression.

- **Title Company:** Essential for ensuring clear property titles and managing the closing process efficiently. They play a critical role in mitigating legal risks by verifying ownership history and ensuring that all the paperwork is accurate and complete. You want someone who will communicate clearly and efficiently with both you and your clients.

- **Insurance Agent, Mortgage Broker, Home Inspector, Appraiser, Landscaper, Handyman, HVAC Technician, Plumber, & Electrician:** Each provides specialized services that enhance the buying and selling process. Even beyond the sale, your clients will reach out for recommendations when renovating or repairing the property they purchased. Having a strong network of professionals is a huge value add and keeps you top of mind.

- **Movers and Packers:** Transitions clients to their new homes smoothly and hassle-free, handling the logistics of moving and packing with care. Again, you want people that are going to handle your clients with as much care as they do their boxes. It does no good if they are good at packing/moving but are rude or difficult to communicate with. This can be an emotional time for many, so ensuring your vendors are handling your clients with care should remain an utmost priority.

- **Legal Advisor or Real Estate Attorney:** Someone specialized in real estate law can help navigate complex legal transactions, resolve disputes, and ensure compliance with all local and federal regulations. They are crucial for drafting and reviewing contracts and handling any legal issues that arise. Knowing an attorney that specializes in FIRPTA (Foreign Investment in Real Property Trust Act) and 1031 Exchanges (Section 1031 of the Internal Revenue Code) will provide the support necessary for international real estate transactions and tax-deferred property exchange.

- **Property Manager:** Whether rental property is an area of focus for you or something you refer out, having a property manager with great customer service can be an invaluable asset and help ensure that if you do pass a referral to a rental company, it makes its way back to you when they are ready to buy.

FUTURE NEEDS:

- **Financial Advisor:** Beyond daily operations, a financial advisor helps you plan for long-term financial health. From investments to retirement planning, they ensure every dollar you earn today is working towards a more secure tomorrow.

- **Sign Installer:** Handles the installation and removal of your real estate signs. Some brokerages do provide this service, and in some cases, agents may even choose to install their own signs. However, when you get busy, this is an affordable piece that is easy to outsource and saves you not only time and gas but, depending on where you are in the country, it can also save you from freezing in the snow or melting in the sun to make it happen.

- **Transaction Coordinator:** Manages documents and ensures smooth transactions. This may be a service provided by your brokerage. If not, you may choose to invest in a transaction coordinator to free up your time from managing paperwork and allow you to go out and procure more leads—whether that be from calling your database or attending a lunch at your local chamber of commerce.

- **Home Stager:** Enhances the appeal of your listings by styling homes in a way that makes them more attractive to potential buyers, often speeding up the sale process and increasing the selling price. The reality is, buyers often can't visualize an empty or over-cluttered space. Hiring a home stager to take that guesswork out of it is a value add for many properties. Beyond listings, these professionals can also help your buyers with home design.

- **Marketing Consultant:** While a graphic designer handles the visual aspects, a marketing consultant can strategize broader marketing efforts, including digital marketing, newsletter content creation, and market analysis to better position your listings and personal branding in the market.

- **Social Media Manager:** As digital presence becomes increasingly important, having someone dedicated to managing your social media accounts can provide consistent engagement, lead generation, and brand visibility. However, keep in mind that in the world of real estate, your socials need to remain hyper local. There are many automated services that are far too general and not area focused that end up not resonating with your target audience and truly become a waste of money. Consider hiring a high school or college student to intern, giving them an opportunity make some cash while building their resume. No matter who you choose, be sure to arm them with your state real estate advertisement requirements.

- **Assistant, Virtual or not:** As your business grows, having a dedicated person or team to handle client inquiries, feedback, and follow-ups can improve client satisfaction and free up more time for you to focus on closing deals.

If you encounter someone impressive but don't yet have a role for them, add them to your vendor list for future reference. With your desired roles filled, your team will not only support your operational needs, but also elevate the entire home buying and selling experience for your clients, ensuring you cover every aspect from listing to closing. Build a team that not only meets expectations, but exceeds them in every way!

BUILDING A UNIFIED TEAM

While skills and experience are undeniably crucial, there's something else that's just as important when building your dream team: culture fit. It's the secret sauce that makes the difference between a good team and a great one. How well your team meshes and collaborates can truly make or break your business.

You've spent a lot of time ensuring you found the right brokerage. When you're assembling your team, you want to take that same care—look for individuals who don't just bring the right skills to the table, but who also resonate with your business values, your work ethic, and your vision for the future. You want to build a team that's in harmony not only in terms of what they can do, but also in how they think and feel about the work they do.

Think about it: a team that shares your passion for providing exceptional client service or your commitment to ethical business practices will be more motivated, cohesive, and effective. They'll be the kind of team that doesn't just clock in and out; they're the ones who go the extra mile because they believe in what they're doing and they know they're valued.

But how do you find these gems? A great starting point is your brokerage. Many brokers maintain a list of core vendors who have proven their reliability and effectiveness in past collaborations. These are professionals already vetted for quality and performance, giving you a solid foundation to build from.

Need more options? Don't hesitate to ask other agents in your office for their recommendations. Their firsthand experiences can provide invaluable insights. However, don't just take a recommendation at face value. Make it a point to reach out personally—set up a call or a meeting. Ask questions that delve into how well these candidates align with your business values, and discuss expectations for future collaboration. This is your opportunity to gauge their compatibility with your vision and ensure that they can truly meet your needs.

Taking these steps helps you not only find skilled professionals, but also form a network of vendors who are truly in sync with your approach to real estate. This thorough vetting process is crucial in building a team that will contribute to your success for years to come.

NURTURING YOUR NETWORK OF EXPERTS

Once you've assembled your dream team of vendors, consultants, and independent contractors, it's crucial to think about how you can deeply invest in these relationships to foster mutual growth and success. Remember, even though they aren't your employees, these professionals are integral to your business's operations and achievements. By investing in their development and creating a supportive network, you not only encourage a culture of continuous improvement, but also create a powerhouse where everyone thrives.

Firstly, consider ways you can provide training or professional development opportunities that are mutually beneficial. For instance, you might host a workshop on the latest real estate trends that includes your favorite mortgage broker, insurance agent, and home inspector. This not only keeps your team up to date, but also keeps everyone aligned with the market's best practices and helps them offer top-notch service to your clients.

Investing in your team also means being open to feedback. Encourage your vendors to share how processes can be improved or how client satisfaction can be enhanced. This not only helps in refining your business operations, but also makes your vendors feel valued and heard, strengthening your professional relationships.

A team that grows together stays together and thrives together—even if it's a network of independent professionals. By investing in their growth, you're not only enhancing their expertise, but also deepening their commitment to your shared success. Together, you can achieve more, reach higher, and truly transform the real estate landscape.

Investing in the growth of your network isn't just good practice—it's smart business. When they succeed, you succeed, and that's a winning strategy for everyone involved.

THE HEARTBEAT OF YOUR BUSINESS

In real estate, as in life, everything comes down to relationships. Open lines of communication aren't just helpful—they're absolutely essential. Think of your team like a well-oiled machine in which every part knows exactly how to move in harmony with the others. This clarity and synchronicity come from ensuring that everyone from your photographer to your closing attorney knows their role, understands the team's goals, and sees how their contributions help paint the bigger picture.

But the magic really happens in the celebration. Real estate is a relationship business, and strong, positive relationships with your vendors can transform them into wonderful sources of referrals. When you take the time to celebrate successes—both big and small—it does more than boost morale; it keeps you at the forefront of their minds. Whether it's a group call to cheer a particularly innovative marketing campaign or a coffee meet-up to celebrate a sale, each celebration reinforces your appreciation and solidifies these crucial business relationships.

Make it a point to acknowledge and honor every win. This could be through a celebratory post on social media, a special mention in your newsletter, or even just a heartfelt thank-you note. Each act of recognition builds a stronger, more connected team. This isn't just about making people feel good—it's strategic. Happy, engaged team members who feel valued are more likely to speak highly of you and refer additional business your way.

Let's keep those communication lines buzzing with positivity and that champagne glass always at the ready. Remember, we're not just building a team here; we're nurturing a community. By fostering a culture that values open communication and shared successes, we're setting the stage for a thriving business built on lasting and fruitful relationships. Here's to working, celebrating, and succeeding together!

> The right path is the one you pave yourself.

3
Your Business Blueprints

Laying Down Your Business Foundations

Ready to roll up your sleeves? As we begin to dive into the essentials of setting up your real estate business, it's crucial to understand that one of the biggest hurdles new agents face is not treating their real estate profession as a true business from the start. Believe me, I have had many discussions over the years with professionals who refuse to slow down enough to acknowledge that they are not only a real estate agent, but a real estate business owner. I know it's wild when you put it in those terms. I also understand that it is so easy to get distracted by the thrill of day-to-day agent-centric tasks like lead generation and market analysis, because let's face it—you didn't become a real estate agent because you wanted to think about business structure.

However, putting all the daunting biz setup on the back burner often leads to a scramble months or even years later to untangle the mess. Imagine building a gorgeous mansion of your dreams on a foundation that didn't have the correct engineering and was being undermined by the stress of the environment. Before you know it, the floor gives way and your dream home crumbles. Yeah—we're not going to let that happen, because we know that in order to run a successful business, we have to treat it like a *business*.

I've witnessed high-producing agents struggle at year-end, frantically trying to compile everything for tax purposes because they failed to set up a proper system from the start. I remember talking with one particular agent about the money she was leaving on the table by not tracking expenses properly or having her businesses set up in a way that best benefited her. Truth be told, getting a system in place after you've been operating a certain way for years becomes so daunting that you will continually put it off, and that's just what she did. But guess what? As she began speaking to a financial planner, she was pressured to make the necessary changes to her business in order to set herself up for the future.

Just know that if you decide to switch business structures later in your career, it impacts everything from bank accounts to credit cards, W-9 forms, taxes, and state licenses. While there may be unique instances where adjustments are necessary, more often than not, if you just take the time to set up a solid foundation from the start, you will save yourself time, money, and stress down the line. Not to mention, set your business up for success.

With this in mind, I've compiled some simple yet critical steps to help you get your business off on the right foot. This isn't just about navigating through paperwork and legal jargon; it's about strategically planning and structuring your business to support sustainable growth and prevent potential pitfalls. Whether you're aiming to operate solo or dreaming of managing a large team, making the right foundational decisions is crucial.

Come on... does it *really* matter? A million times YES! Setting up your real estate business correctly from the beginning is essential for several reasons:

1. **Legal Compliance:** Each state has its own set of rules and regulations governing real estate practices. Proper setup ensures that you comply with these laws, which can vary widely from one state to another. Compliance is not only about avoiding legal mishaps, but also about protecting your reputation and your business's longevity.

2. **Financial Management:** Starting with a solid financial plan and the right accounting practices can save you from future financial strain. Proper financial setup helps you track your income and expenses accurately, manage cash flow efficiently, and plan for taxes effectively. It's about establishing systems that will help you make informed decisions and scale your business without losing control of your finances.

3. **Operational Efficiency:** A well-structured business runs more smoothly. This means having the right tools, systems, and processes in place to handle client management, listings, transactions, and marketing. These systems not only help you manage your daily tasks more efficiently, but also free up your time to focus on growing your business and serving your clients better.

4. **Risk Management:** The right business structure and insurance can protect your personal assets and provide a safety net for unforeseen circumstances. Whether it's choosing between an LLC or a sole proprietorship or deciding on the type and amount of insurance you need, these decisions play a critical role in risk management.

5. **Professional Image:** How you set up your business also impacts how clients and peers perceive you. A professional setup reflects your commitment to your career and can build trust with your clients and credibility within the industry.

THE FRAMEWORK OF YOUR SUCCESS

When selecting the right business structure for your real estate venture, think of it as choosing the type of home that best suits your lifestyle and needs. Just like homes, each business structure offers different levels of complexity, protection, and flexibility. This decision is crucial, which is why consulting with a tax and/or legal professional is highly recommended. However, let's explore a few options so you can understand why this decision is so important.

SOLE PROPRIETORSHIP

A sole proprietorship is like a cozy studio apartment—compact, straightforward, and easy to manage. This structure is ideal if you're venturing into real estate solo and prefer to keep things simple. While it offers the convenience of easy management with minimal overhead, remember that in this setup, your personal and business assets are *not* separated. This means there is greater exposure to personal liability.

LIMITED LIABILITY COMPANY (LLC)

A Limited Liability Company (LLC) can be compared to a townhouse equipped with protective bylaws. It offers more room and flexibility than a studio apartment and comes with the added benefit of personal asset protection, similar to community rules that protect all residents. This structure shields your personal assets from business liabilities, allowing you the freedom to operate with less risk. It's ideal for those who want the liability protection typically associated with larger business structures but with less formality and more operational flexibility.

PROFESSIONAL LIMITED LIABILITY COMPANY (PLLC)

A Professional Limited Liability Company (PLLC) is similar to an LLC but designed for licensed professionals.

Like a specialized townhouse within a specific community, a PLLC offers similar protections and benefits as an LLC but is tailored for professionals who must meet certain state-specific requirements. This structure is ideal for real estate professionals looking for liability protection while still adhering to the regulatory standards of their profession.

PROFESSIONAL ASSOCIATION (PA)

A Professional Association (PA) is like a house in a gated community—it's structured, secure, and offers substantial protection for its residents, in this case, the business owners. This setup provides strong protection from personal liability and features that can help raise capital, such as the ability to issue stock. However, like living in a gated community with strict rules and higher maintenance costs, a PA requires compliance with regulatory requirements and involves more complex operations and tax obligations.

Choosing the right business structure is like picking the perfect home—it must suit your current needs while also accommodating your plans for future growth. Each structure, much like different types of homes, comes with its own set of benefits and responsibilities, making it essential to carefully consider your options. Consulting with a legal or financial professional can offer vital clarity and guidance, ensuring that the structure you choose not only provides a strong foundation for your business, but also aligns with state-specific requirements. This decision is fundamental, affecting everything from your day-to-day operations to the potential expansion of your business.

FINANCIAL FOUNDATIONS

Oh, the classic saying: "You have to spend money to make money." Trust me, it's never more true than when you're kicking off your career as a real estate agent. Right out of the gate, you're shelling out for your real estate classes, fingerprinting, prep courses, study materials, the state exam, and maybe you even found yourself adopting a furry friend to serve as your emotional support animal through the whole process. But, my friend, that's just the warm-up. Up ahead? There are local, state, and national dues, MLS fees, business cards, headshots, yard signs—oh my!

Tracking your expenses is super important, and it can be a bit of an adjustment—especially if you're usually the type to tell the cashier to keep the change.

Let's talk about setting up smart money management practices right from the start because, believe it or not, they're key to growing and sustaining your real estate business effectively. So, what does this look like in real life? Think about setting up bank accounts, diving into spreadsheets, investing in some accounting software, and maybe snagging a company credit card.

Once you've decided on the best structure for your business, the next move is to open a business bank account to keep things smooth. This account is like that dedicated nook in your home where magic happens—it keeps your business finances neat and tidy, separate from your personal funds, ensuring everything runs smoothly. Opening a separate business account also simplifies your bookkeeping and tax prep by keeping all your business-related money in one spot. If you're really on the ball, why not open two accounts? One for your regular biz expenses and another just for taxes. That way, when payday rolls around, you can squirrel away what you owe Uncle Sam right off the bat.

Now, let's chat about investing in some accounting software. This is basically your business's financial HQ, giving you the lowdown on your financial health at a glance. Good accounting software will help you track your income, manage expenses, keep an eye on profit margins, and handle tax liabilities. It's your best friend for dodging financial stress and making sure your business isn't just surviving but thriving.

Did you know that some MLS fees might cover accounting software? For instance, my MLS uses a product called Hurdlr, which doesn't cost me any extra money. But heads up: things like this can change, since MLS contracts and offerings tend to evolve. So, there might come a day when you'll need to budget for this out of your pocket. A lot of financial pros love QuickBooks, just FYI.

If your MLS doesn't offer anything for accounting and your budget is super tight, start simple. A basic spreadsheet for tracking money in and out, paired with a folder in a cloud-based system like Google Drive or Dropbox to store all your scanned receipts, can work wonders. Seriously, as long as you're consistently recording and organizing every penny, you're setting yourself up like a pro.

Also, let's not forget about creating a budget that reflects both what you need right now and your dreams for the future. Think of it as your business's nutrition plan—it's what keeps your business healthy and pumped for growth. A smart budget helps you anticipate costs, plan for investments, and manage your cash flow so you can grab opportunities as they come and even weather the slow seasons without breaking a sweat.

Many new agents don't see their first commission check for anywhere from six to twelve months. Crazy, right? There are a bunch of factors that play into this—like how long it takes to snag a lead and then actually get them to the closing table. You've got to build up a pipeline that keeps feeding you, so in the beginning, you might see money flowing out pretty steadily with none coming back for a while. This is exactly where your budget steps in to save the day and set you up for success.

So, when you get your license and you're over the moon—shout it from the rooftops! But maybe hold off on splurging on that billboard unless you've got a special stash set aside for it. "Budget" might sound like a buzzkill word, but let's reframe it: it's your strategy for success. There's a reason why only a fraction of agents make it past the first couple of years and money is often a main factor.

So, what should you budget—I mean, "strategize"—for? It varies a lot depending on what your brokerage offers and charges you for. If you haven't already, chat with some local agents to see where they put their money at the start, what was worth it, and what they wish they'd skipped. We'll dive in deeper in Chapter 4, but some key categories to consider when you're first starting are licensing and education costs, association and multiple listing service (MLS) fees, marketing and branding, office and technology expenses, transportation costs, insurance and legal fees, operational costs, networking and professional development, and an emergency fund.

While you're diving into setting up and fine-tuning your financial systems, remember, you don't have to go at it alone. It's super smart to bring a financial advisor or accountant on board who really knows the ins and outs of real estate. Think of them as your financial fairy godparent, someone who's there to sprinkle a little magic on all things money management.

These pros are not just number crunchers; they are seasoned navigators of the real estate financial waters. They come armed with a wealth of specific knowledge and can offer advice that's tailored just for you and the unique challenges you might face in the real estate industry. Whether you're dealing with fluctuating market conditions, complex property investments, or even your everyday income and expenses, they know what's up.

But their expertise doesn't stop there. They can help you develop sophisticated strategies that could potentially save you big bucks down the line. We're talking tax planning that maximizes your deductions and minimizes liabilities, all while keeping you within the bounds of the law. And speaking of laws, staying compliant with the ever-twisty maze of state and federal regulations is no joke. It's crucial for keeping your business on the up and up, legally and financially sound.

Investing in a financial expert is one of those moves you won't regret. It's an investment in making smart, informed decisions that safeguard your business and set you up for long-term success. With the right financial setup, you're not just surviving in real estate; you're *thriving*.

TURNING BIG IDEAS INTO REALITY

Think of your operational plan as the secret sauce that transforms your big dreams into even bigger realities. It's all about piecing together systems that make your daily grind as sleek and impactful as possible. We're going to unpack each system in Chapter 8, but before we dive in, here's a little sneak peek to get you pumped.

Client Management System: Kick off with a top-notch Customer Relationship Management (CRM) system. Think of it as your super-efficient, never-sleeping personal assistant. It remembers every little detail—from each client's birthday to their favorite coffee and the last deal you discussed. A stellar CRM system keeps all your client interactions on record, helping you deliver a personalized experience that makes every client feel like the MVP. This kind of attention can turn even first-timers into lifelong devotees.

Listing Management: Craft a methodical approach to manage your listings like a pro. This spans from snapping breathtaking photos that showcase your properties in the best light and organizing open houses that are sure to draw in crowds, to keeping your listings fresh and updated across all platforms. Effective listing management ensures every property shines and is marketed perfectly, skyrocketing your chances of a swift sale at a top dollar.

Marketing Strategy: Whip up a marketing strategy that marries traditional tactics with digital savvy. Use eye-catching flyers and bold signage to catch the eyes of passersby. Amp up these efforts with dynamic social media campaigns, engaging email blasts, and a sleek, easy-to-navigate website to reel in online audiences. Your aim is to stitch together a unified marketing plan that spreads your brand and offerings far and wide, ensuring maximum visibility across all channels.

Feedback and Adjustments: Remember, a killer operational plan is always evolving—it thrives on feedback and actual results. Regularly assess how well your systems and strategies are performing. Are your clients happy? Are properties flying off the market as quickly as you hoped? Use client insights and sales data to tweak and fine-tune your approach, continuously pushing for higher efficiency and better outcomes.

Team Collaboration and Tools: If you're part of a team, ensure everyone's on the same wavelength with the right collaborative tools. Whether it's through shared calendars, project management software, or instant messaging apps, the right tools can elevate team productivity and make sure nothing slips through the cracks.

Training and Development: Lastly, dedicate time for ongoing training and development for you and your team. The real estate landscape is ever-changing, and staying on top of new trends, tools, and regulations is key to keeping your edge. Whether it's getting a handle on the latest real estate laws, mastering new marketing techniques, or getting savvy with emerging tech, continuous learning is a crucial component of your operational playbook.

By building a thoughtful and flexible operational plan, you're not just aiming to meet your goals—you're setting the stage to surpass them. This blueprint is about more than just keeping things tidy; it's about forging a system that lets your real estate business flourish and pivot with the ever-shifting market. Let's put this plan into motion and watch your business soar to new heights!

> Achievements are built on a foundation of perseverance.

4

Mastering Commissions & Cash Flow

A Guide to Smarter Financial Practices

Ready to whip your finances into shape? Think of this chapter as your personal finance workout—no sweatband required. We're diving deep into the essentials, breaking down the must-know financial lingo, setting up a budget that feels good, and strategizing to keep your cash flow healthy.

UNDERSTANDING REAL ESTATE COMMISSIONS

First things first: let's clear up some common myths about how real estate agents get paid. If you haven't bought a home before or you're new to the real estate world, you might think agents earn a base salary or possibly a small hourly wage on top of commission. In reality, real estate agents typically earn their income purely through commissions. And let me tell you, what they end up taking home has to pass through a few hoops before landing in their bank accounts!

COMMISSION BASICS

Real estate commissions are usually calculated as a percentage of the property's sale price. This is all negotiated up front, nice and clear, through either a listing agreement with a seller or a buyer brokerage agreement with a buyer. These contracts are super important because they outline the commission rate that will compensate you for all your hard work during the transaction. Whether you're marketing a listing or negotiating like a pro, these agreements ensure that your efforts are rewarded.

Here's how it all goes down:

- **Commission Agreement:** Picture this: you're about to show some amazing properties to a potential buyer, but first, you get down to business by negotiating your commission. This happens when you sign a buyer brokerage agreement, setting clear expectations right from the start. The same goes when you're working with sellers—before that "For Sale" sign goes up, you'll have agreed on your commission rate by entering into a listing agreement. And get this: sometimes during negotiations, a seller might even offer to cover the buyer's agent's commission as a sweet buyer incentive.

- **Sale of Property:** When that property finally sells, the commission you and the buyer's agent agreed upon is calculated from the final sale price. It's payday at closing, my friend!

- **Brokerage Split:** Here's where it gets a bit technical, but stick with me. The commission you worked so hard for? Well, it gets paid directly to your broker, and then they pay you according to the terms you've agreed upon. This could include a split of the commission, corporate fees, transaction fees—you name it. Make sure to double-check your brokerage agreement to see exactly what you can expect to come your way.

- **Final Payout:** After all your hard work, you'll see your take home. From this portion, you'll need to cover your operating costs (we'll dive into those juicy details soon) and smartly tuck away about 20-30% for taxes. Tax planning might not be glamorous, but it's totally necessary. And hey, when in doubt, chatting with a CPA can really clear up the muddy waters of tax obligations.

Understanding how your commission checks flow isn't just a cause for celebration—it's essential for strategically planning and growing your business. Each real estate transaction comes with its unique nuances and, depending on where you are, regional norms that can influence how commission structures are set up. This makes having a crystal-clear agreement and mutual understanding between all parties involved not just helpful, but absolutely crucial.

The actual percentages and how they are split can vary widely. Factors like brokerage standards, the complexity of the deal, and negotiations between the involved parties all play a part. Getting a grip on these details does more than just prepare you for a nice payday—it lays the foundation for effective business planning and scaling. By truly understanding this process, you can set realistic goals, anticipate future earnings, and tailor your strategies to maximize every opportunity.

SMART BUDGETING

Okay, let's dive into budgeting—a word that might make you think of endless spreadsheets and a little bit of dread. But what if I told you we're about to flip the script and turn budgeting into something you might actually look forward to? We're going to align it perfectly with your real estate hustle and those inevitable income fluctuations that come with the territory.

BUILD A FLEXIBLE BUDGET

Imagine this: some months, you're closing deals like a rockstar DJ spins tracks—everything's upbeat, and the cash flows effortlessly. But then there are those quieter times, when the market takes a breath—and so does your income. This is where crafting a flexible budget comes into play. By tucking away a portion of your earnings during those peak months, you create a financial cushion that softens the quieter periods. It's like choreographing a dance where some moves are high-energy and others are slow and steady, but all are perfectly in sync, keeping your finances beautifully balanced.

I've put together a general overview of what a budget may look like. But keep in mind that there's no one size fits all when it comes to business and money.

INCOME

As a real estate agent working primarily on commission, your income might feel like it's on a rollercoaster—some months are up, soaring with successful closings, and others might dip lower than you'd like. It's crucial to get a handle on this ebb and flow early on. To start, base your income estimates on industry averages for your area—this gives you a ballpark figure to work with while you're building up your own sales history.

Think about crafting a range that includes both your champagne-popping, celebration months and those tougher times when things are quieter. This approach helps you paint a realistic picture of what you can expect financially. It's all about preparing for the highs and bracing for the lows, ensuring you're never caught off guard.

FIXED EXPENSES

These are costs that remain relatively stable from month to month, including:

- **Association Dues**: Typically, annual fees for local, state, and national Realtor associations.

- **MLS Fees:** Monthly or annual fees for access to Multiple Listing Services and lockbox access.
- **Insurance:** This includes professional liability (errors and omissions insurance) and possibly health insurance, if not provided through another family member's plan.
- **Office Rent/Desk Fees:** If applicable. Review your brokerage agreement to confirm if any desk fees are required.

VARIABLE EXPENSES

These expenses can fluctuate based on your level of activity and need to be closely managed:

- **Marketing and Advertising:** Costs for online ads, printed materials like flyers and signage, business cards, website maintenance, professional photography and videography, and social media promotion.
- **Travel and Transportation:** Fuel, car maintenance, public transportation costs, and possibly a car payment if you use a vehicle primarily for work.
- **Client Entertainment and Gifts:** Expenses for dining out with clients, closing gifts, etc.
- **Continuing Education and Licensing:** Costs for classes to meet continuing education requirements and renewal of your real estate license.
- **Technology and Tools:** Subscription costs for CRM (Customer Relationship Management) software, data

services, and other tech tools that help manage client relationships and streamline operations.

- **Networking and Professional Development:** Fees for joining networking groups and costs associated with attending industry conferences, seminars, and workshops.

OPERATIONAL COSTS

- **Equipment and Supplies:** Computers, smartphones, cameras for property photos, and office supplies.
- **Professional Services:** Fees for accountants, lawyers, or consultants.

SAVINGS AND INVESTMENTS

It's crucial to allocate a portion of your income to savings for:

- **Emergency Fund:** Aim to have at least three to six months' worth of expenses saved, given the variability of real estate income. This is crucial for longevity in this industry. We will dive deeper into this later.

- **Retirement Savings:** Contributions to a retirement account or another vehicle appropriate for self-employed individuals. I highly recommend consulting a financial advisor to help guide you on how to put your income to work for you. Nearly 40% of agents do not adequately plan for retirement. Shocking, I know!

- **Tax Savings:** A percentage of each commission set aside for taxes to avoid surprises come tax season.

Setting up and sticking to a well-thought-out budget is like mapping your route to success in the real estate world. It helps you manage your finances with finesse, covering all those essential expenses while paving the way for your future growth and stability. Think of your budget as your business's GPS—it keeps you on track, no matter where your real estate journey takes you.

Now, let's talk strategy. When you work with a client, what does it actually cost you? It's not just about the big stuff. Every coffee meetup, every stunning photo you commission to showcase a property, each targeted ad you run on social media, and those thoughtful closing gifts—all these add up. So, how do you plan for them? Start by setting a standard for each type of expense. Knowing what you typically spend will help you create a budget that truly reflects your business operations.

Consider these questions: How often will you treat clients to coffee? What kind of photography and videography packages do you need to make your listings pop? What's your budget for social media ads per listing? How lavish are those closing gifts going to be? Pinning down these numbers gives you a clear picture of your spending and helps you allocate your resources more effectively.

Here's the deal: your budget isn't set in stone. It's fluid and adaptable. While you can't plan for everything (because let's face it, surprises are part of the game in real estate), you can certainly prepare for a lot. Being prepared isn't just a good idea in business; it's essential to thriving in this bustling market.

So, let's get your finances feeling good, looking good, and performing even better. Your budget isn't just numbers on a spreadsheet; it's the backbone of your business strategy, designed to carry you from here to your dream destination in the real estate world.

BUDGET MANAGEMENT

- **Track Your Spending:** Let me say it louder for the people in the back: TRACK. YOUR. SPENDING. Use budgeting apps or that accounting software we talked about earlier to keep a detailed record of *all* business-related expenses. Get with your CPA/accountant on which chart of accounts you should use for your business. A chart of accounts is a list of all the financial accounts used to categorize and record your transactions (money in and out), providing an organized overview of your financials.

- **Review Regularly:** Given the variability in income, it's important to review and adjust your budget monthly. You'll want to look at your advertising costs and see what business you generated from those efforts in order to decide whether or not to make that financial investment again in the future.

- **Plan for Slow Periods:** Use good months to prepare for slower times, ensuring you have enough reserves to cover your fixed expenses.
- **Optimize Tax Deductions:** Yup, I'm going to say it again... **track your spending.** Keep meticulous records of all deductible expenses to minimize your tax liability.

EMERGENCY FUND

All right, let's dive into one of the unsung heroes of your financial toolkit: the emergency fund. Setting aside enough to cover three to six months of essential expenses can truly transform your approach to personal finance. This isn't just another savings account; it's your financial peace of mind in a bank.

I've seen it more than I care to admit—real estate agents forced to go back to their bartending days or desk jobs, building someone else's dreams just to make it through. While I'm all for hustling to make ends meet, imagine the market takes a nosedive, or an out-of-the-blue expense pops up—situations no one wants—but you don't have to hit the panic button. Instead, you've got a built-in financial buffer that allows you to navigate through unexpected storms without capsizing your budget.

It's about more than just having money stashed away; it's about maintaining your lifestyle, keeping your stress levels in check, and protecting your future plans. Building this fund might sound daunting, but you can start small. Each commission check is an opportunity—set a part aside and watch your safety net expand. Over time, you'll find this fund isn't just a cushion; it's a launchpad that gives you the confidence to make bold moves and take calculated risks, knowing you have a solid financial fallback.

So, why not start today? Begin weaving your safety net, one thread at a time, and turn potential financial freefalls into graceful landings. Go ahead, take a moment and transfer what you can into your new emergency fund—whether it be $1 or $1000. Think about it: you can start funding your emergency fund today, right now even—a true cornerstone of your real estate career!

INVEST FOR GROWTH

Here's the exciting part: when you nail a fantastic month (and trust me, you will!), what's next for that extra cash? Let it sit and gather dust? Absolutely not. You put that money to work! Investing in opportunities like retirement accounts, real estate ventures, or other financial instruments means your money doesn't just sit back and relax—it's out there hustling, growing, and expanding, just like you. We're not just saving here; we're strategically boosting your wealth, ensuring every dollar you earn is working towards building a more prosperous future.

The idea of investing can be daunting and might even feel out of reach at times. But remember that financial advisor we added to your dream team? This is where they shine. Bring them into the game, and let them outline what's possible for you in the short and long term—one, five, ten, even thirty years down the road if you start planning now.

DEMYSTIFYING FINANCIAL STATEMENTS

All right, so you've got your budget outlined, your emergency fund is in the works, and you've started exploring investment opportunities. But how do you keep track of all this financial progress? Let's dive into something that might sound a tad intimidating but is actually your secret weapon in mastering your finances: understanding financial statements. Yep, we're talking about balance sheets and profit and loss statements. These aren't just dreary grids of numbers; they're like the storybooks of your business, narrating where your money's been and forecasting where it's headed.

Each line on these statements tells a part of your business's financial story, giving you insights into your financial health and guiding you towards smarter financial decisions. So, let's turn those intimidating reports into tools that empower you to write a successful financial future.

BALANCE SHEETS

Think of a balance sheet as a snapshot of your financial health at any given moment. It's like taking a selfie of your business finances! This snapshot will show you three key things:
- **Assets:** These are what you own. It could be cash in the bank, investments, office equipment, or even that snazzy new laptop you just bought for your real estate work.

- **Liabilities:** These are what you owe. Think of things like credit card debt, loans, or maybe even that balance you're still paying off on your car.

- **Equity:** This is the magic number that shows what's truly yours after subtracting your liabilities from your assets. It's like taking a snapshot that shows the true value of what you've built.

PROFIT AND LOSS STATEMENTS

Now, onto the profit and loss statement, or as I like to call it, your business' report card. This document tells you exactly how well your business is performing over a specific period —be it a month, a quarter, or a year. Here's what it covers:

- **Revenue:** This is your total earnings from selling your real estate services. It's every penny that comes in from closing deals and any other services you provide.

- **Expenses:** These are all the costs you incur to run your business. Advertising, client coffees, gas for all those property viewings—you name it.

- **Profit:** This is what's left after you subtract your expenses from your revenue. It's the true measure of your business's success in that period.

Understanding these statements can feel like you're translating a foreign language, but once you get the hang of it, you'll see they offer invaluable insights. They help you pinpoint where you're making money, where you might be overspending, and how you can keep improving your financial health.

WHY DOES IT ALL MATTER?

Getting cozy with your balance sheets and profit and loss statements means you're no longer just running your business day-to-day; you're strategically planning for its future. You'll see opportunities to cut unnecessary expenses, reinvest in areas that are doing well, and ultimately, drive your business towards more profitability.

If you're anything like me, reviewing your profit and loss statement becomes a bit of a treasure hunt. Each time, there's almost always an expense lurking that you can trim—whether it's by tens, hundreds, or even thousands. It turns into a strategic game: How can I cut costs without compromising the quality of service or missing out on opportunities? It's all about finding that sweet spot where efficiency meets excellence, ensuring every dollar spent is truly an investment in your business's growth.

Reviewing a Profit and Loss (P&L) Statement and a Balance Sheet regularly is essential for several reasons:

1. **To Monitor Financial Health:** The Balance Sheet gives you a snapshot of your business's overall financial condition at any given point in time, including what assets you own and what liabilities you owe. It helps you gauge your company's stability and liquidity.

2. **To Track Profitability:** The P&L Statement shows how much money your business has made and spent over a specific period. Reviewing this helps you understand if you are operating at a profit or loss. This insight is crucial for measuring the effectiveness of your business strategies and operational efficiency.

3. **To Make Informed Decisions:** Regular reviews of these financial statements provide the data you need to make informed business decisions. For example, understanding your cash flow can influence decisions on hiring, marketing investments, expansion, and other significant expenditures.

4. **To Identify Trends and Patterns:** Analyzing these statements over time can help you spot trends and patterns in your business operations. For instance, you might identify seasonal fluctuations in income or particular areas where expenses can be cut.

5. **For Tax Preparation:** Accurate and up-to-date Balance Sheets and P&L Statements are crucial for tax preparation. They ensure that you report your financial situation accurately to tax authorities and can help in maximizing deductions and avoiding penalties for misreporting.

6. **To Attract Investors or Loans:** If you're seeking investment or need to apply for business loans, these financial statements will be required by potential investors or banks as proof of your business's financial health and potential for growth.

Regularly reviewing your P&L Statement and Balance Sheet not only keeps you informed about the financial status of your business, but also guides you toward sustainable growth and success.

Who ever said budgeting had to be a bore? With this approach, you're not merely managing your money; you're orchestrating a financial strategy that moves in sync with the natural highs and lows of the real estate market. Tune your finances to harmonize with your ambitions, making sure each dollar is carefully choreographed and every financial decision hits the mark. Here's to turning budgeting into an exhilarating part of your thriving real estate career!

> Seek environments
> that inspire and
> support you.

5

Navigating Real Estate Taxes & Laws

Essential Insights for Every Real Estate Professional

Taxes and laws might seem as fun as a root canal, but they're absolutely vital to keeping your real estate business running smoothly and legally. We're going to break it all down into digestible, pain-free pieces—promise! This chapter is your friendly guide through the potentially intimidating world of real estate regulations and tax requirements. While reviewing taxes and laws can be a bit of a snoozefest, it's important for your success—so just hang in there with me and we'll get through it together. Let's dive in, so we can make sure you're not just compliant, but confident and well-informed.

MAKING TAX SEASON A BREEZE

Oh, tax season—just the thought can send a shiver down the spine of even the most seasoned real estate pros. But what if I told you that with a little preparation and organization, you could handle tax time like a boss? Here's your guide to navigating taxes with grace and, believe it or not, a bit of ease.

DEDUCTIONS AND EXPENSES

First things first: Deductions are your best friends. From office supplies and mileage to home office setups and marketing expenses, every penny counts. We've talked about the how—keeping meticulous records by investing in a good system for tracking expenses throughout the year, whether it's an app, spreadsheet, or good old-fashioned filing system. Now let's chat about the why—the better your records, the easier it is to claim every deduction you're entitled to, maximizing your potential savings when taxes roll around. More deductions = less money to Uncle Sam.

QUARTERLY TAXES

As an independent contractor, the IRS expects you to pay quarterly estimated taxes if you're pulling in a decent income. Waiting until April to pay your taxes in one lump sum? Not the best idea. It could lead to penalties and interest from our not-so-forgiving friend, the IRS. Setting calendar reminders to make those quarterly payments is not just a good practice; it's a stress reducer. This is also where your real estate dream team comes in and you can rely on the advice of your CPA/accountant when those payments are due.

CAPITAL GAINS

A lot of people become an agent so they can invest in real estate without having to pay out commission. If selling personal properties is part of your business model, you've got to have a handle on capital gains tax. This tax applies to the profit from selling properties that have gone up in value since you bought them, and the rates depend on how long you've held onto a property. Knowing the difference between short-term and long-term capital gains rates can significantly affect your financial strategy and tax liabilities. Keep tabs on your hold periods and consult with a tax and/or legal professional to strategize the best times to buy and sell.

HIRING A TAX PROFESSIONAL

Given the complexities of real estate transactions and the steep penalties for slip-ups, a tax professional who's well-versed in real estate tax law is a must. They can navigate the murky waters of things like pass-through deductions and the impacts of the Tax Cuts and Jobs Act on real estate pros. Think of them as your financial co-pilot, steering you clear of potential tax pitfalls and toward tax savings.

Jessica Souza

NAVIGATING REAL ESTATE LAWS

Real estate laws vary widely from state to state, and even local regulations can differ at the county and city levels. While I'm not an attorney and won't be diving into specific legal jargon, consider this your essential crash course. It's designed to highlight areas you should investigate further—perhaps with the help of a local legal expert from your real estate dream team.

Here are some key legal areas every real estate professional should be familiar with:

DISCLOSURE OBLIGATIONS

Navigating your disclosure obligations might sound a tad technical, but let's break it down into real-talk, especially for those of us braving the beautiful but stormy Sunshine State. Yes, Florida is as gorgeous as they come, but with those stunning views comes a fair share of high winds and surging storms. You'd be surprised at what some homeowners might try to cover up or "forget" to mention when it comes to property damages or regular flooding.

We've had sellers who experienced water intrusion on a regular basis—they knew it, their neighbors knew it. Heck, the mold mitigation company knew it. They had water come in from a storm prior to listing the property for sale, failing to disclose this to their listing agent. When the inspection results came back, the inspector had noted that there were some mold spores. One call to a mitigation company for a quote revealed that the sellers had called for a quote themselves and never moved forward with mitigation—they decided to sell instead. Needless to say, crisis averted for those buyers. It is situations like this that remind us to ask all the questions, even if you think it isn't applicable to that property. Let them tell you that—don't ever assume.

Here's a pro tip: Arm yourself with a rock-solid intake form for listings and a comprehensive list of questions for listing agents when you're representing buyers. These forms ensure that nothing critical is "accidentally" overlooked. We're talking about asking all the tough questions—because when it comes to your clients' new home, there's no such thing as too much information.

Trust me, any little omissions or hidden issues are bound to come out eventually, usually discovered by the new owners when they least expect it. And let's be real: if those new owners end up dealing with unexpected surprises, they're not just going to be upset—they might take legal action. And guess who's likely caught in the middle? Yep, that could be you, having to prove that you knew nothing about it.

That's exactly why robust disclosures are your best friends. They do more than just cover the legal bases—they build trust. By ensuring that every significant detail is disclosed upfront, you're not just protecting your clients; you're also safeguarding your own reputation as a thorough and caring real estate pro. Not to mention, certain insurance policies won't cover you if the necessary disclosures aren't used. So let's keep it open, honest, and completely transparent. In real estate, the best policy is always to lay all the cards on the table—ensuring every transaction is clear.

CONTRACT LAW ESSENTIALS

Diving into the basics of real estate contracts can really empower you as an agent, ensuring every agreement you facilitate is legally binding, crystal clear, and fair. This includes coming to grips with purchase agreements, listing agreements, lease agreements, and buyer's broker agreements—all of which are the backbone of transactional integrity in real estate.

Here's the thing: Contracts can vary wildly. You might encounter specific state forms, local board of Realtor forms, brokerage forms, builder forms, or even DIY contracts penned by someone who'd rather not hire a professional. As I've mentioned before, I'm no attorney—and chances are, you aren't either. It's crucial to understand the terms of these agreements and the role you play in executing them, but remember, your job isn't to provide legal explanations.

As a real estate agent, your role involves walking through the contract with your clients and helping them understand the terms they are setting or agreeing to. Fill out the contract entirely—those empty spaces and checkboxes are often required, not optional, and by leaving them blank, your client could be agreeing to default terms. Become familiar with the disclosures available to you and when to use them. If they have questions or need more detailed explanations about the legal language used, it's wise to recommend that they consult an attorney.

I've been on the receiving end of an agent explaining a contract and the information provided was... let's just say, not quite on the mark. Fortunately, it didn't affect the transaction, but it could have—and everyone might not be so lucky. The realm of contract law is complex, which is exactly why some professionals dedicate their careers to it. We don't need to be contract law experts ourselves. Our expertise should be in real estate, knowing the ins and outs of properties, markets, and client needs, and recognizing when it's time to hand over the reins to the legal experts for further clarification.

Navigating this with caution not only protects your clients, but also shields you from potential legal entanglements. Always aim to be the expert in real estate who knows when to step back and let the legal professionals take the lead on the intricate details of contract law.

UNDERSTANDING PROPERTY TAXES

All right, let's tackle a topic that might make your eyes glaze over just a tad—property taxes. But stick with me, because getting a handle on this is like unlocking a superpower in the real estate world. Knowing the ins and outs of property taxes isn't just helpful; it's essential for providing your clients with top-notch service and setting clear financial expectations from the get-go.

You've learned how these taxes are calculated in your pre-licensing course. But what goes into determining these tax rates? It's not just about your property's size or style; it's also about where it's located. Local governments set tax rates based on the budget needs of various public services, like schools, parks, and emergency services. That means property taxes can vary widely from one neighborhood to another, even within the same city, depending on local funding needs.

Understanding property taxes is crucial because it directly affects homeowners' budgets. For your clients, this isn't just a line item on their bill; it's a significant annual or semi-annual expense that can influence their decision on whether a home is right for them. Higher property taxes might mean a bigger monthly budget, especially if taxes are escrowed into mortgage payments, which is often the case.

I've encountered situations where a property appeared to have negligible taxes at a glance—but that was because it had been homesteaded and was benefiting from tax exemptions due to the owner being a disabled veteran. However, after the property changed hands, the exemptions were removed and the property was reassessed, leading to a more than doubled tax bill. Fortunately, the agent involved was well-versed in the nuances of property taxes and the timing of tax reassessments, so the new owners were fully prepared for the increase. This is why it's crucial to have a thorough understanding of the property taxes they might face in their new home. It helps prevent surprises and ensures they are financially prepared for their investment. Moreover, if they're comparing properties in different areas, understanding how taxes influence overall costs often becomes a major deciding factor.

NAVIGATING PERMITS AND ZONING

Let's dive into the world of permits and zoning. Navigating this space is like mastering a crucial part of the real estate puzzle, and trust me, you want to get it right.

UNDERSTANDING THE BASICS OF ZONING

First up, zoning laws. These are like the rule books that dictate what you can and can't do on a property. Zoning laws affect everything from the type of buildings that can be constructed to the activities that can take place within those buildings. I've seen folks buy property without fully understanding these regulations, only to discover they can't open their dream business or that their new home is next to a future multi-family development. Whether you're dealing with residential, commercial, or mixed-use areas, understanding these laws is key to planning any property development or improvement and guiding your clients to make a good investment that fits their needs.

And then there are zoning disputes—nobody's favorite scenario, but they do happen. Disagreements might arise over property boundaries, permitted uses, or compliance issues. Knowing how to handle these situations can save a ton of headaches. Often, this involves negotiations with local authorities or even presenting your case before zoning boards. While most of the time you might not handle these disputes directly, being aware of the process allows you to direct your clients to the right contacts to address their concerns effectively.

WHY PERMITS MATTER

Next, let's talk permits. Permits are the green light that let you proceed with your plans. They're necessary for most construction projects, major renovations, and even some types of landscaping work. Why? Because they ensure that your project complies with local building codes, safety standards, and, yes, those zoning laws. The requirements can vary significantly, even from one municipality to another within the same region—so getting to know the specifics for your service areas is crucial.

Navigating the permit process can feel daunting, but it's all about knowing where to go and what to ask. You'll typically start at your local building department or zoning office. Here, you can gather all the details about the permits you need, the documents you should provide, and the fees you might have to pay. And remember, be patient and kind—these office staff are just doing their jobs, enforcing rules they didn't make.

WHY IT ALL MATTERS

Understanding permits and zoning isn't just bureaucratic hoop-jumping, though it can feel a lot like it. It's about being a savvy agent who knows the ins and outs of the process so you can navigate it clearly yourself and, of course, provide the proper guidance to your clients. Whether you're checking permits on the new window install for your next possible listing or verifying if the new roof on the home your buyers like was done to code, mastering this area ensures that you can inform your clients so they are able to make educated decisions on some of the biggest investments of their lives.

FAIR HOUSING AND ANTI-DISCRIMINATION

Okay, let's take a moment to focus on something super important—actually, it's essential. Remember those Fair Housing laws you skimmed over in your pre-licensing course, noting which ones were enacted in which years? Well, diving into the specifics of those laws might seem like just another item to tick off your to-do list, but trust me, it's much more profound than that. These aren't just rules to follow; they reflect our deep commitment to fairness and equality in every aspect of our business.

Here's the deal: whether we're talking federal, state, or local levels, fair housing laws are meticulously designed to prevent discrimination in real estate transactions. This means decisions in our industry should never be based on race, color, religion, sex, disability, familial status, or national origin. But this goes beyond just avoiding discrimination; it's about actively creating an inclusive and welcoming environment for all our clients. It's more than passing a test or ticking a box—it's about being a genuinely good human.

Let's set the standard high and lead the way. It's crucial that we thoroughly understand these laws not only because we're required to, but because it's simply the right thing to do. We're in a position to make everyone feel at home, not just in their new property but in how they're treated, from the first hello to the final handshake. Let's be the agents who don't just follow the rules, but who also create a space where everyone feels valued and respected.

ETHICAL AND PROFESSIONAL STANDARDS

All right, let's dive deep into ethics in real estate—a topic that truly goes beyond mere compliance. This is about who we are as professionals and how we build trust with our clients, our brokers, and our peers in the industry.

For many of us, acting honestly and fairly is just second nature. But navigating the complexities of real estate transactions isn't always easy. That's why maintaining high ethical standards is like having a GPS for your career—it guides you to stay on the right path. It's about more than just sidestepping pitfalls; it's about actively building a reputation that draws clients and other professionals who are eager to work with someone they can trust. Ethical conduct ensures that you're not just closing deals but doing so rightly, focusing on fairness and respect for everyone involved.

Your reputation is undoubtedly one of your most valuable assets. In real estate, word of mouth can either be your best marketing tool or your biggest challenge. Upholding strong ethical standards helps protect your professional image, establishing you as both reliable and full of integrity. Picture this: agents skipping showing certain properties simply because the seller wasn't offering cooperating compensation. Such decisions aren't ours to make; our clients deserve the chance to see all relevant properties. When clients see your commitment to ethical practices, they feel more secure in their dealings with you, which can lead to repeat business and glowing referrals.

But this isn't just about us as individuals; it's about our industry as a whole. By sticking to high ethical standards, we boost the overall integrity of the real estate profession. We set an example that lifts the entire field, influencing how the public views all real estate professionals and shaping the future of our industry. Let's embrace these principles, not only to safeguard our careers, but to ensure that the real estate profession remains respected and trusted by everyone.

And there you have it—your crash course on navigating real estate taxes and laws! With your newfound knowledge and skills, you're not just ready to take on the real estate world; you're set to thrive in it. Now, go out there and apply what you've learned, and make every transaction count. Remember, every deal, every client, and every closed sale is not just a business win—it's a stepping stone to becoming the kind of real estate pro who doesn't just succeed but truly shines. Here's to your future, where the only way is up!

> Surround yourself
> with those who
> lift you higher.

6

Finding Your Ideal Client

A Guide to Ethical Targeting

Who's your dream client? I know, that sounds like a simple question. But I challenge you to really dig deep. Identifying your ideal client is all about blending understanding with strategic marketing. We're not casting wide nets here; we're crafting smart, targeted strategies that perfectly align with who you want to serve. And we're doing it all while firmly adhering to Fair Housing laws and wrapping every action in integrity and inclusivity.

Why Specialize? Think of it like this: just as you'd seek out a specialist for a specific health issue, your clients are seeking a specialist for their unique real estate needs. You wouldn't visit a cardiologist for a broken foot, right? Likewise, clients prefer real estate agents who specialize in exactly the type of help they need. While it might be tempting to try and serve everyone, doing so can spread you too thin, leading to stress and diluted results.

Instead of casting a wide net, focus on attracting the types of deals and clients that align with your expertise and passion. This strategic approach not only reduces stress, but also enhances your effectiveness. By honing your outreach and services, you create a clearer, more compelling brand message that resonates deeply with the clients you're most equipped to help.

Pinpointing Who They Are: Create a detailed client persona to guide your marketing efforts. For instance, meet Sarah and Tom, a young couple eager to buy their first home. They're tech-savvy, environmentally conscious, and in search of a sustainable living space within walking distance to urban amenities. On the other hand, consider Carlos, a retiree aiming to downsize to a tranquil, suburban locale close to parks and health care—emphasizing low-maintenance, accessible living.

By clearly defining who you are serving, your marketing becomes more focused and effective. You'll attract clients like Sarah and Tom, or Carlos, who will benefit most from your specialized knowledge and approach.

Here are a handful of questions designed to help you zero in on your dream clients in real estate. Think of this as creating a detailed profile for your ideal buyer or seller. By understanding their unique needs and desires, you can tailor your approach to connect deeply and effectively.

1. **What stage of life are they in?** Are they newlyweds looking for their first home, growing families in need of

more space, or retirees looking to downsize? Each stage brings its own set of priorities and challenges.

2. **What's driving their move?** Are they seeking a new job, closer proximity to family, better schools for the kids, or a lifestyle change? Understanding their "why" can help you provide the most relevant options.

3. **What neighborhoods or types of properties are they drawn to?** Do they dream of quaint suburban neighborhoods, vibrant city blocks, or peaceful rural retreats? Are they condo hunters or searching for sprawling estates?

4. **What does their financial picture look like?** Knowing their budget and financial comfort zone can help you guide them to the right properties without stretching their finances too thin.

5. **What features are on their must-have list?** Are they looking for sustainability features, a home office, a big backyard, or walkability to local amenities? Pinpointing these desires can narrow your search and boost your efficiency.

6. **How tech-savvy are they, and what's their preferred communication style?** Do they embrace technology and prefer digital documents and virtual tours, or are they more traditional, appreciating phone calls and paper?

7. **What's their timeline for this transaction?** Are they in a rush to move because of a new job or a baby on the

way, or are they more relaxed and flexible about their timing?

8. **How do they like to receive information?** Would they love detailed emails full of stats and properties, or do quick texts and highlights work better for them?

9. **What lifestyle factors are important to them?** Think about what matters most in their daily lives: is it the commute to work, access to parks and recreation, or the local coffee scene?

10. **What were their previous real estate experiences like?** Understanding their past dealings can help you enhance their current experience. Did they feel supported and listened to, or are there areas they're hoping to improve?

While you may not know the answer to every question, this exercise not only helps you understand your clients on a deeper level, but also positions you as a caring, attentive real estate professional who's all about personalizing the experience. Let's make each client relationship as unique and special as the homes they're seeking!

CRAFTING MESSAGES THAT CONNECT

Once you've pinpointed who your ideal clients are, it's time to craft messages that not only reach, but deeply resonate with them. This isn't just about promoting properties; it's about forging real connections and building trust. It's showing that you get their unique needs and dreams, and you're here to turn those into reality. Your communications should make them feel seen and understood, like you're the real estate matchmaker they've been searching for.

By fine-tuning your approach to specifically address your demographic, you do more than meet expectations—you dazzle them. You elevate your business from one-size-fits-all to bespoke brilliance, making every interaction meaningful and every client feel exceptionally valued. Let's not just find the right clients; let's deeply connect with them, leading to successful transactions and shining referrals.

EXAMPLE CAMPAIGN:

SOCIAL MEDIA STRATEGY:

- For Sarah and Tom, design a series of Instagram stories highlighting eco-friendly homes, complete with green certifications and quick tips on living sustainably. Sprinkle in client testimonials that rave about their new, eco-conscious lifestyles.

- For Carlos, create LinkedIn posts that tour accessible homes, focusing on safety features, ease of access, and serene neighborhoods perfect for peaceful retirements.

EMAIL MARKETING:

- To engage first-time buyers like Sarah and Tom, send a monthly newsletter filled with insights on eco-friendly housing trends, sustainable living tips, and spotlight features on the latest green homes on the market.

- For those looking to downsize like Carlos, craft emails that discuss how to tailor a home for accessibility and convenience, including links to properties that embody these ideals.

Crafting effective campaigns for your target clients isn't just about knowing the basics; it's about taking the time to understand their needs, desires, and lifestyle preferences. Here are some follow-up questions based on our previous exercise. They're designed to help you tailor your marketing campaigns perfectly to resonate with your demographic. Let's get to the heart of what makes your clients tick and create messages that truly speak their language!

UNDERSTANDING YOUR CLIENT

1. **Who is your ideal client?** Describe them in as much detail as possible (age, occupation, family size, lifestyle interests, etc.).

2. **What are their primary goals in buying or selling a home?** Are they first-time homebuyers, upsizing for a growing family, downsizing, or investing?

3. **What challenges do they face in the real estate process?** How can you address these challenges through your services?

4. **What are their hobbies and interests?** How can these insights shape the types of homes and neighborhoods you recommend?

CRAFTING YOUR MESSAGE

1. **What values resonate with your target client?** How can you reflect these values in your messaging?

2. **What type of content do they engage with most on social media?** (e.g., videos, blogs, infographics, testimonials)

3. **What fears or concerns might they have about the real estate process?** How can you alleviate these in your communications?

BUILDING CAMPAIGNS

1. **Outline a potential social media campaign for your target client.** What platforms will you use, and what content will you create? Include themes or specific post ideas.

2. **Design an email marketing strategy.** What kinds of information will you include in your newsletters? How often will you send them?

3. **What traditional marketing methods (if any) would appeal to your target client?** (e.g., mailers, billboards, local newspaper ads).

EVALUATING SUCCESS

1. **How will you measure the success of your campaigns?** Consider metrics like engagement rates, click-through rates, lead generation, and conversion rates.

2. **What feedback process will you put in place** to learn directly from your target clients about what works and what doesn't?

By dialing into your demographic using these targeted, thoughtful approaches, you're not just reaching out to potential clients—you're inviting them into a conversation that feels personal, relevant, and respectful. This is how you build lasting relationships in the real estate world, ensuring your message isn't just heard, but resonates deeply. Let's make sure every interaction is as personalized and impactful as possible, setting you up as the go-to agent for your dream clients!

INTERACTIVE WORKSHOPS

Imagine creating a space where potential clients don't just hear about the housing market, but actively engage with their dreams. Hosting interactive workshops provides a perfect space for just that. These sessions are more than informative—they're dynamic experiences where your clients can get their hands dirty (figuratively, of course!) and dive deep into what really lights them up about finding a home.

For Sarah and Tom, envision a workshop titled "Green Homes 101: Finding Your Sustainable Dream Home." This session could explore everything from eco-friendly materials and energy-efficient designs to the latest in sustainable living innovations. Enhance the interaction with a virtual tour of a green home, or bring in a guest speaker who specializes in eco-conscious architecture.

For Carlos, consider "Navigating Your Next Move: Downsizing with Ease," focusing on practical tips for selecting the right smaller space, decluttering, and adapting to a compact lifestyle. A guest expert in senior living or a professional organizer could provide invaluable insights and hands-on advice.

These workshops do more than inform; they empower. You're providing personalized learning experiences that build knowledge and confidence. Plus, they're a fantastic way to forge deeper connections, establishing trust and demonstrating that you're genuinely invested in supporting their journey from start to finish.

LEVERAGING YOUR REAL ESTATE DREAM TEAM

Your real estate dream team brings these workshops to life! Involve your trusted mortgage broker to demystify financing, or your go-to home inspector to reveal the ins and outs of property evaluations. They're not just there for support; they're key players who enhance the learning experience with their expertise, ensuring attendees receive comprehensive, firsthand insights.

Imagine your landscaper sharing tips at the "Green Homes 101" workshop on creating sustainable outdoor spaces, making the concept of eco-friendly living fully tangible. For Carlos's session, a downsizing expert could demonstrate how to streamline living spaces effectively, making transitions smoother and more manageable.

Each workshop is a dynamic event that educates, engages, and builds a sense of community among attendees. It showcases your network of professionals as accessible, knowledgeable, and integral to the real estate process, elevating your clients' experience and solidifying your reputation as a resourceful, connected agent.

TIMING IS EVERYTHING

Timing isn't just a piece of the puzzle; it's often the piece that can mean the difference between a message that fizzles out and one that sparks action! Leveraging the power of analytics, we get to play detective, uncovering those golden hours when your audience is most active and engaged online. This isn't about guesswork; it's about using data to make smart, strategic decisions that put your messages right where they need to be—at the forefront of your potential clients' minds when they're most receptive.

Think about it: you wouldn't want to send out an exciting new listing announcement at four a.m. when everyone's asleep, right? Instead, using insights from social media and email analytics, we can identify peak times when your particular audience is scrolling through their feeds or checking their emails. For instance, maybe your target demographic tends to engage most during lunch breaks or in the evening hours after work. Those are your windows of opportunity!

Here's how we make it happen: by setting up scheduled posts and emails to go out during these optimal times, you ensure maximum visibility and engagement. This strategic placement increases the chances that your content doesn't just get seen—it gets interacted with, driving more traffic to your listings, boosting your profile, and ultimately helping you build those crucial relationships with potential buyers and sellers.

Harness the power of timing to make sure your well-crafted messages don't just reach your audience, but truly resonate with them. It's about being seen at the right place and the right time, making all your marketing efforts count. Get strategic and watch as your engagement rates not only climb, but soar!

STAYING COMPLIANT AND INCLUSIVE

As we hone in on identifying your target clients, it's absolutely crucial to integrate Fair Housing principles into every facet of our campaigns. This isn't just about adhering to legal obligations—it's about elevating our ethical standards and showcasing our unwavering commitment to fairness in every post, every ad, and every interaction.

Use language that speaks universally, focusing on what truly matters to your clients—their dreams and needs. By consciously avoiding phrases that could hint at demographic biases, we ensure that everyone feels seen, understood, and valued.

EMBEDDING FAIRNESS IN YOUR MARKETING

DO:

- Regularly review your marketing materials to ensure they comply with Fair Housing laws.

- Educate yourself and your team on the nuances of these laws to avoid unintentional violations.

DON'T:
- Use language that could be perceived as exclusionary or indicative of a preference for or against any group based on race, color, religion, sex, disability, familial status, or national origin.
- Make assumptions about what a client may want based on their background. Always base your guidance on explicit preferences and needs expressed by the client.

By embedding these practices into your marketing strategies, you're not just selling properties—you're building a brand that stands for trust, inclusivity, and ethical integrity. Let's ensure your marketing efforts resonate deeply and respectfully with everyone. This is how you forge lasting connections and build a legacy that transcends transactions. Here's to making your real estate practice a beacon of inclusivity and trust!

> Lay a foundation strong enough to build dreams on.

7

Creating a Brand That Connects

Make Your Mark Unforgettable

Hey there, lovely! Think about this: every single day, our choices—like what we wear, what car we drive, where we shop, and even the food we pick up—are touched by branding. It's powerful, right? When I sit down with agents eager to carve out their professional niche, I often hear, "It's just a logo, isn't it?" But oh, how much more it is! Your brand? It's not just a logo. It's the heart and soul of your business, the very essence of your being in the marketplace.

Remember that client profile we worked through in the last chapter? Now think about the kind of experience you want to create for them. What's the vibe you want them to feel during and after they connect with you? This chapter is your ultimate guide to digging deep and articulating those core values that make your brand uniquely, authentically you. We're going to infuse your entire business with your essence, making sure your brand does more than just exist—it resonates deeply and leaves a lasting impression on your dream clients.

Refining your brand goes beyond a pretty logo—it's about crafting a real representation of your mission and values. It's about being seen and felt, making your brand not just a part of the conversation, but a memorable part of your clients' lives. Let's dive into this journey together, not just to create an image, but to build an identity that captures hearts and minds.

DISCOVERING THE HEART OF YOUR BRAND

So, let's pause for a second and focus right at the core—YOU. This is where the magic starts. We're not just skimming the surface; we're going deep to unearth the real, brilliant you. Who are you in this bustling market? What unique strengths do you bring to your clients? This isn't about fitting into a mold; it's about breaking the mold to showcase a brand that's unmistakably yours.

We'll kick off with some soul-searching exercises that peel back the layers of your professional persona. What drives you? What are your absolute must-have values? By answering these questions, you start to sketch a vivid picture of what makes you stand out. This isn't just an exercise; it's the unveiling of your true self.

Ready to dive deep and discover how to make your real estate brand speak volumes before you even say a word? Trust me, it's going to be amazing!

EXERCISE: CRAFTING YOUR REAL ESTATE BRAND

If you're new to the whole branding scene, this exercise is just for you. When you join a brokerage, you are one of dozens, hundreds, or maybe even thousands of agents within the brokerage's brand. How are you going to stand out amongst the rest? It's all about discovering and defining a unique identity that will help you sparkle in the real estate world. We're going to dive deep into who you are, what you stand for, and how you want your dream clients to see you. Let's simplify this into fun, manageable steps.

Step 1: Define Your Core Values. First things first: what exactly are core values? Think of them as your business's guiding stars, the ones that light up your path in this wild career journey. They're not just fancy words for your website; they are the soul of your biz and the heart behind every decision you make.

Caught at a crossroads? Your core values are like your inner compass, whispering which way to go, making sure it's the way that feels most "you." Whether it's being totally transparent, passionately creative, or putting your clients first, these values are the framework of your journey.

Why does this matter? Because when you're crystal clear about your core values, you're not just running a business—you're creating a brand that feels like a second home. You attract the kind that truly resonate with your unique flair and make decisions with confidence. It's about crafting an experience that's as beautiful on the inside as it looks on the outside.

Ready to start? Grab a cozy spot and jot down your thoughts on these questions:

- What values are you absolutely not willing to compromise on?
- What traits do you admire in others?
- Reflecting on your successes, what values were you embracing?

From your answers, highlight five core values that sing to your heart—these are going to be the core of your brand. This isn't just busy work; it's the foundation of how you'll stand out and truly connect in the real estate market. Let's make your brand not just seen but felt, in a way that's completely, authentically you.

When you're diving into the heart of your real estate brand, think about the values that sing to your soul and resonate with how you do business every day. Here are a few values you might consider weaving into your brand's identity, values that go beyond the basics and really speak to who you are:

- **Integrity:** Stick to honesty and fairness in every deal. It's not just about doing things right; it's about doing the right things.

- **Dedication:** Be all in for your clients, always ready to go the extra mile to make their dreams come true.

- **Innovation:** Embrace the new and nifty—whether it's the latest tech or a fresh way to solve old problems, you're there to make things better.

- **Community Focus:** Connect with your community. It's about more than just houses; it's about helping the whole neighborhood thrive.

- **Transparency:** Keep it crystal clear. From listings to closings, make sure every step is understandable and open.

- **Reliability:** Be the rock your clients can lean on, no matter what time it is or what they need.

- **Empathy:** Tune into the emotions involved in every transaction. Show your clients you truly get what they're going through.

- **Professionalism:** Uphold the highest standards in every interaction. Show the world what it means to be a pro.

- **Respect:** Honor every client's time, needs, and wishes as if they were your own. No matter the size of the deal, every client is a big deal.

- **Sustainability:** Champion green practices in real estate to help our planet. It's all about leaving things better than you found them.

Choosing values like these isn't just about setting standards; it's about making a promise to every person you work with that they're getting the real you in every transaction. These values should sparkle through every facet of your business, from your marketing all the way to your day-to-day client interactions. Let's make your brand not just seen but felt, creating an experience that's as genuine as you are.

Step 2: Pinpoint Your Strengths. Okay, now it's time to dive into what makes you shine! Think about what you do better than anyone else and how that can make a world of difference for your clients. Reflect on the sweet words from past clients, coworkers, or mentors—what do they always say you're great at? Jot down those unique skills and qualities that set you apart from the crowd. Now, pick the top three superpowers you think will truly resonate with your dream clients. This isn't just about being good; it's about being uniquely you.

Step 3: Visualize Your Ideal Client. Remember that ideal client we dreamed up? Let's bring them into clearer focus. Who are they really? What are they looking for in a home or a real estate experience? Sketch a quick profile of them—think about their demographics, lifestyle, and what they're aiming for in the real estate world. Now, let's line up your core values and strengths with their needs and dreams. This is where your unique abilities meet their unique needs.

Step 4: Create Your Vision Board. Let's get visual! Create a board that captures the essence of your brand and the vibe you want to send out into the world. Pull together images, quotes, and symbols that speak to your core values and strengths and reflect the spirit of your ideal client. You can go digital with Pinterest or old-school with a corkboard —whatever sparks your creativity. Look for patterns that emerge—these will be the guideposts for your brand's style and messaging.

By tackling these steps, you're not just building a brand; you're crafting an identity that's as vibrant and genuine as you are. This clear vision won't just market your business—it will magnetize the right people who are just waiting to find someone exactly like you. Let's break away from the ordinary, forge a brand that's 100% you, and watch as it transforms not only your business, but how you feel about every single day you work. Create an experience so compelling that your clients can't wait to jump on board with what you're doing.

CRAFTING YOUR MISSION

Think of your mission statement as the heartbeat of your brand. It's not just a catchy sentence; it's the powerful declaration of your passion and purpose. This is your chance to articulate the impact you strive to have on your clients and the community. It's about defining the deeper "why" behind every listing you take on and every home you help to buy.

Here's the beautiful part: your mission statement gives your brand its soul. It guides your business decisions, influences your marketing strategies, and aligns your goals. Whether you're aiming to empower first-time homebuyers with knowledge and confidence, or you're committed to helping families find their forever homes, your mission should reflect the essence of what you do and why you do it.

Creating a powerful mission statement can significantly impact how clients perceive and engage with a real estate agent. Here are a couple of examples followed by a simple formula you can use to craft your own:

"Empowering clients to achieve their dreams of homeownership through dedicated service, personalized guidance, and unwavering integrity."

This statement emphasizes empowerment, personalized service, and integrity, appealing to clients who value support and ethical dealings.

"To transform the real estate experience by fostering community and building trust, ensuring every client feels confident and valued throughout their journey."

This focuses on transforming experiences, building community, and instilling confidence in clients, targeting those who seek a relationship-driven approach.

A STEP-BY-STEP GUIDE

- **Action Verb**: Start with passion! Choose a strong verb that leaps off the page and captures the essence of your activities. This verb should reflect your "why"—the core reason you're in this business. Whether it's to **empower, transform, innovate, simplify, guide,** or **assist**, pick a verb that pulses with energy and commitment.
- **Target Audience**: Who are your dream clients? This is the group of people you identified in the last chapter that you are most passionate about helping. Whether it's first-time homebuyers who are navigating the complexities

of the market, families looking for their forever homes, or investors seeking lucrative opportunities, knowing your audience helps tailor your mission to their specific needs and aspirations.

- **Service/Value Proposition**: What unique offerings do you bring to the table? This is where you shine a light on your unique services that meet the needs of your audience. Are you offering unparalleled market insights, stress-free transaction processes, or maybe customized, client-focused solutions? Highlight your strengths here.

- **Desired Outcome/Impact**: Envision the finish line—what impact do you aim to have on your clients and your community? This could be helping them achieve the dream of homeownership, ensuring they feel valued and supported, or helping them build a secure financial future with wise property investments. Your mission should encapsulate the positive change you strive to create.

By aligning these elements, your mission statement will not only define what you do, but also inspire and attract the people you're meant to serve. It's about making your professional promise guide every business decision and client interaction.

Formula to Create Your Mission Statement:

[Action Verb] + [Target Audience] + [Service/Value Proposition] + [Desired Outcome/Impact].

Example Using Formula:

[Guide] + [first-time homebuyers] + [through simplified, educational transactions] + [to confidently achieve their dream of homeownership].

Putting it All Together:

"Guide first-time homebuyers through simplified, educational transactions to confidently achieve their dream of homeownership."

This formula helps ensure your mission statement is clear, memorable, and impactful, encapsulating the essence of what you aim to achieve in your real estate career.

Remember, your mission statement is your banner in the marketplace. It's what you rally behind and what you want others to remember about you. Create a mission that not only tells the world what you stand for, but also inspires you every day to give your best.

YOUR UNMISTAKABLE SIGNATURE

Picture this: in an ocean of real estate agents, your voice is like a lighthouse—it's what guides clients to your shore. It's not just about being heard; it's about being recognized, being relatable, and being remembered. Whether it's the empathetic tone in your emails, the enthusiastic energy of your property tours, or the insightful posts you share on social media, every word and every interaction should scream "you."

This section is all about crafting a voice that feels like home to your clients. Your voice is your brand's heartbeat, pulsing through your website, echoing in your videos, and whispering through your blog posts. Here's how we'll uncover the unique tone, style, and key messages that make your brand pop.

1. **Discover Your Tone**: Are you the friendly neighborhood expert? The savvy investor's go-to? Or maybe the compassionate guide for first-time homebuyers? Your tone will dictate how clients feel about your brand. It could be warm and inviting, professional and authoritative, or fun and energetic. Think about how you naturally communicate and how your clients respond to it.

2. **Define Your Style**: Your style is how your voice is visually and textually represented. It's the words you choose, the fonts on your website, the colors in your branding. It's the casual jeans-and-tee vibe or the tailored-suit formality that you bring to your video content. Your style should align with your tone to present a cohesive brand image.

3. **Craft Key Messages**: Remember the core messages you want to consistently communicate. These could be about your dedication to client satisfaction, your deep understanding of the market, or your commitment to ethical practices. Your key messages are your brand pillars; they support every campaign, every post, and every client meeting.

4. **Authenticity Rules**: In a world where everyone is trying to sell something, authenticity wins. Don't be afraid to let your real personality shine through. People want to

do business with *people*. They can tell when you're genuine, and a sincere voice will build trust faster than any sales pitch.

5. **Consistency is Key**: Once you find your voice, stick with it across all platforms. Consistency helps build familiarity, and familiarity breeds trust. Whether someone visits your Instagram, reads your newsletter, or browses your website, they should feel like they are encountering the same person each time.

Over time, you won't just find your voice—you'll refine it into a powerful tool that enhances your brand and builds deeper connections. Turn your voice into your ultimate real estate superpower, making every word count and every interaction meaningful.

CONNECT, CAPTIVATE, AND CONVERT

All right, you've sculpted a brand that's as authentic as it is appealing, mirroring your unique vibe and vision. Now, let's turn that brand into a client magnet, drawing in those dream clients who aren't just looking for any agent—they're looking for *you*.

This is all about harnessing the power of your well-defined brand to not only attract, but also deeply connect with your ideal clients. It's not about casting a wide net; it's about casting the right one. Here's how to make sure your brand resonates with those who will appreciate and seek out your specific approach and expertise.

1. **Targeted Marketing Magic**: Create marketing strategies that speak directly to your ideal demographic. Whether it's through hyper-local SEO (search engine optimization), curated content on social media, or direct mail that feels personal and relevant—every piece of your marketing puzzle should fit perfectly into the lives of your target clients. Explore which platforms they frequent, what messages they respond to, and how to make your marketing feel like a warm, welcoming conversation instead of a sales pitch.

2. **Community Engagement**: Embed yourself in the communities where your ideal clients thrive. Sponsor local events, host informative real estate workshops, or volunteer in initiatives that matter to you and your audience. By showing up, not just as an agent but as a community member, you create a natural attraction. People want to work with someone who doesn't just work in their community, but actively contributes to and cares for it.

3. **Consistent Content**: Use your blog, podcast, or YouTube channel to share content that resonates with your ideal clients. If you're targeting eco-conscious families, share tips on sustainable living or spotlight green homes on the market. For urban professionals, focus on lifestyle content that highlights the convenience and vibrancy of city living. Your content should be a resource that they can't wait to consume and share.

6. **Referral Ripples**: Happy clients are your best advocates. Encourage satisfied clients to share their positive experiences by providing easy ways for them to spread the word online and offline. Remember, a referred client comes with built-in trust, significantly shortening the sales cycle.
7. **Feedback Loop**: Always seek feedback from clients to refine your approach continuously. Understanding what resonates with them or where gaps might exist helps you tweak your strategy to better meet their needs. This not only improves client satisfaction, but also turns casual clients into loyal advocates.
8. **Visual Cohesion**: Ensure that your visual branding is on point across all touchpoints. From your business cards and signage to your social media profiles and listing presentations, every visual element should echo your brand's core identity. This visual cohesion builds brand recognition, making your brand memorable and instantly identifiable.

By focusing on these strategies, you're not just attracting clients; you're attracting the right clients. Those who resonate with what you stand for will naturally gravitate towards you, creating not only business opportunities but also relationships built on shared values and mutual respect. Make your real estate practice a magnet for your ideal clients, turning every meeting into a potential partnership. Here's to filling your client list with names that energize and inspire you!

> Understand your worth and plan accordingly.

8

Operating with Excellence

Tools and Techniques for Enhancing Your Operational Efficiency

Operations are totally my jam—I thrive on crafting streamlined systems. I'm constantly on the hunt for new ways to not just boost efficiency, but to enhance productivity, which inevitably leads to increased profitability over time. I've watched as agents, team leads, and even brokers have hesitated to integrate technology into their businesses, or have chosen systems that don't quite meet their needs. Unfortunately, this often results in wasted time and money as they struggle to patch up the shortcomings of their existing processes.

In this book, we're not just going to check tasks off a list—we're going to completely transform how you approach your work. Get ready to elevate your business to a whole new level of awesome! We'll make sure you're equipped with the right tools and know-how to avoid the pitfalls of inadequate systems and instead, thrive with operations that are as efficient as they are effective. Let's get your real estate business humming like a well-oiled machine!

EMBRACING TECHNOLOGY

First up, let's dive into the tech world—because, let's face it, the right technology can completely transform your workday from overwhelming to manageable. We're not just talking about any tech here; we're focusing on smart, intuitive tools designed to streamline your operations and supercharge your productivity.

In real estate, we categorize our daily operations into two main buckets: front office and back office. The front office includes your IDX (Internet Data Exchange) website, CRM (Customer Relationship Manager), and marketing tools. These are your client-facing systems that drive engagement and help convert leads into sales. Then there's the back office. This is where the magic of transaction management, e-sign capabilities, commission management, reporting, and analytics happens. These systems support the back end of your business, ensuring that everything runs smoothly from contract to close.

With so many options on the market, one of the hardest parts is deciding which system will be the best fit. Let's break down each section of the front and back office systems for clarity and discuss key factors to consider when deciding what systems make the most sense for you and your business.

FRONT OFFICE SYSTEMS:

- **IDX Website:** This is your customer-facing property site. It's where potential clients interact with listings fed from a live MLS feed and get their first impression of your services. An effective IDX website is visually appealing, easy to navigate, mobile friendly, and optimized for converting visitors into leads.

- **CRM System:** A dynamic CRM system keeps all your client details, communication logs, and transaction histories in one accessible place. Whether you're scheduling follow-ups, tracking client preferences, or managing leads, a robust CRM system acts like your personal assistant—one that never takes a day off. This technology makes sure that no client is forgotten and every follow-up is timely, enhancing your efficiency and attentiveness.

- **Marketing Tools:** Essential for promoting your listings and brand, marketing tools range from email marketing to social media ads. These tools help create and distribute engaging content that attracts and retains clients. Whether it's launching a targeted ad campaign or sharing valuable content with your network, these tools ensure your marketing efforts are as effective as possible, maximizing exposure and engagement.

BACK OFFICE SYSTEMS:

- **Transaction Management:** Imagine a tool that keeps every detail of your transactions organized. That's what a solid transaction management system does. It tracks deadlines, manages documents, and handles compliance without breaking a sweat. This system allows you to stay on top of everything effortlessly, ensuring no detail is missed and every transaction is seamless.

- **E-sign Capabilities:** In today's fast-paced market, being able to close deals digitally is non-negotiable. E-sign tools make document signing a breeze, cutting down the waiting time and eliminating paper clutter. They keep the process moving swiftly and securely, so you can finalize agreements faster than you can say "Sold!"

- **Commission Management:** Let's talk money management—specifically, how you get paid. Commission management tools automate the splitting and tracking of commissions. They keep the financials clear and straightforward, so you can easily see what's coming in, what's going out, and how your hard work is paying off. It's about making sure every dollar is accounted for, so you can plan your finances with precision.

- **Reporting and Analytics:** Knowledge is power, especially when it comes to understanding your business's performance. Reporting and analytics tools give you the insights you need to make informed decisions. Want to know how much you paid in desk fees, or what you made first quarter vs. second? These tools provide the answers in clear, easy-to-understand reports, helping you strategize and adjust your business tactics effectively.

- **Mobile Capabilities:** Let's not overlook the power of mobile apps. These gems allow you to manage your business wherever you are, from viewing property details and sharing listings with clients to signing contracts digitally and accessing real-time data. Mobile apps mean that you can be at a showing, in a coffee shop, or on vacation and still have your office at your fingertips. They embody the ultimate flexibility, ensuring that you're always connected and in control, no matter where your real estate adventures take you.

By weaving these front and back office systems into your daily operations, you lay a solid foundation for success, ensuring every aspect of client interaction is handled with care and precision. Many brokerages and MLS systems offer tech solutions as part of their fee structure, which can be a great starting point. Before diving in, though, it's wise to thoroughly evaluate what these products offer compared to others on the market.

While it might seem convenient to go with systems included in the fees you're already paying, there are a few key considerations to address before fully committing:

- **Customization and Scalability:** Does the system grow with your business, and can it be customized to meet your specific needs? You want a system that not only fits your current operations, but also adapts as your business expands.

- **Integration Capabilities:** How well does the system integrate with other tools you are using or plan to use? Seamless integration between systems can significantly boost your efficiency and reduce the chances of encountering technical issues.
- **Support and Training:** What level of customer support and training does the provider offer? A system is only as good as the support behind it, especially when you encounter challenges or need to train new team members.
- **Data Ownership:** Who owns the leads and data that you input into the system? This is crucial, because your data is a valuable asset. Confirm there's a clear agreement with your brokerage that you retain ownership of your data, and check if there's an easy method for exporting data should you decide to change platforms down the line. In a perfect world you would never change brokerages or systems. However, that isn't reality. Whether you're relocating or a system becomes obsolete, you need to be prepared for change. Having the flexibility to move your data without hassle, preserving the integrity and continuity of your client relationships, is extremely important. Your database is one of your most valuable assets in real estate.

Taking the time to clarify these aspects can save you from investing in a system that might not be the best fit for your business long-term. Choosing the right technology should enhance your operations, not complicate them. Let's make sure we're picking tools that not only fit into our budget, but also propel our business forward, making our daily grind smoother and more productive.

ENSURING EXCELLENCE IN EVERY TRANSACTION

Creating a standardized process for all client types—whether they're buyers, sellers, etc.—doesn't just streamline your operations; it makes sure every client experiences the same stellar level of service. To help you craft an exceptional client journey, here's a blueprint of processes tailored for buyers and sellers. This guide is designed to ensure that no matter who comes through your door, they receive thoughtful, thorough, and consistent support every step of the way.

FOR BUYERS

Contact Phase

- **Kickoff with Connection:** Begin with a heartfelt consultation to truly grasp your buyer's needs, preferences, and financial scenario. It's about crafting an atmosphere where they feel valued and heard right from the start. Talk less, listen more, and be sure to take plenty of notes to refer back to.
- **Tip:** Pop their details into your CRM to keep everything organized and at your fingertips.

Pre-Approval Guidance:

- **Navigating the Numbers:** Assist buyers through the mortgage pre-approval maze. This not only clarifies their purchasing power but also signals to sellers that they mean business, smoothing the path to finding their dream home.
- **Tip:** Refer to your dream team mortgage broker and organize all essential documents, like pre-approval letters, in your back office system for easy access.

Home Searching:

- **Finding the Perfect Match:** Leverage your IDX website and MLS to pinpoint homes that tick all the boxes for your clients. Coordinate showings and share your insights on each property, helping them visualize their future. Be prepared to update and refine their search as they explore areas and get a deeper understanding of what they want and need in a property.
- **Tip:** Have a buyer agreement in place before you start the property tours to keep things professional and protected.

Offer to Purchase:

- **Crafting the Offer:** When your client zeroes in on their dream home, assist them in formulating a compelling offer. Discuss market trends and strategic pricing so their bid is both competitive and reasonable.

- **Tip:** Keep your back office loaded with all necessary documents and checklists to ensure nothing slips through the cracks.

Negotiations to Contract:

- **Mastering the Negotiations:** Lead the negotiation process, aiming to secure the best possible terms for your client. Once terms are agreed upon, streamline the signing process using your back office e-sign tools for a seamless experience.
- **Tips:** Review contract terms thoroughly. In the words of my biz partner, Brian Faro, "If it is not in the contract, don't expect it at closing." Once executed, you'll want to coordinate closely with your brokerage, lender, and title company for compliance and smooth dealings.

Pending Phase:

- **Inspection Insights:** Oversee home inspections to identify any issues. Aid in addressing these concerns, keeping the timeline and contingencies in check.
- **Tips:** Utilize your real estate dream team for inspector recommendations and ensure all inspections are scheduled and managed efficiently. If you negotiate credits and/or repairs, not only do you always want to get it in writing, you always want to get it executed by all parties.

Prepping for Closing:

- **Navigating the Closing:** Walk your clients through the closing process with care and competence, making them feel confident and supported at every step.

- **Tips:** Update clients on important aspects like utility connections, insurance options, and home warranty details, keeping them informed and prepared.

Final Walk-Through and Closing:

- **Sealing the Deal:** Conduct a meticulous final walk-through with your clients to confirm every condition has been met. At closing, simplify the paperwork so everything is flawless.

- **Tips:** Arrange a memorable closing gift and confirm your commission with your closing agent prior to closing day.

Post-Closure:

- **Beyond the Sale:** Celebrate the closing, but keep the relationship flourishing. Continue engaging with your clients, ensuring you remain their go-to real estate expert.

- **Tips:** Send a heartfelt thank-you note, request feedback or a testimonial, and share the celebration on social media to enhance your visibility and connection. Continue to look for ways to be a resource beyond the sale.

By embracing this detailed, caring approach, you not only elevate the buyer's experience, but also cement your reputation as a thoughtful and dedicated real estate professional. Let's make every transaction not just successful, but truly special!

FOR SELLERS

Let's transform the process for sellers into a seamless and memorable journey, just like we did for buyers. Here's how we'll make each phase for your sellers as smooth and supportive as possible.

Contact Phase:

- **Kickoff with Connection:** Start with a heart-to-heart consultation to dive deep into your seller's goals and how they envision the selling process. This is your chance to set a warm, supportive tone right from the start and truly understand their "why."
- **Tip:** Pop their contact info into your CRM to keep all the details neat and tidy.

Marketing and Listing:

- **Listing Like a Pro:** Once you've secured the listing, get that property listed with flair using your IDX website and MLS, making sure it pops in all the right places to catch the eyes of eager buyers.
- **Tip:** Streamline the paperwork by creating a transaction in your back office system once you have the address, adding in the required listing documents and any supplemental documents the sellers provide.

- **Marketing Magic:** Whip up a marketing storm with everything from stunning flyers to catchy social media posts. It's all about making that listing shine and stand out from the crowd.
- **Tip:** Launch a "Just Listed" campaign that includes everything from social media blasts to direct mail postcards.

Negotiation to Contract:
- **Offer Handling:** When offers start rolling in, guide your sellers through the negotiation process, ensuring they feel confident and connected every step of the way.
- **Tip:** Document every detail in your back office system to keep the deal moving smoothly and transparently. If you haven't already, this is a great opportunity to provide a net proceeds sheet to compare offers.
- **Sealing the Deal:** Get that contract signed with ease, leveraging your e-sign tools to make the process smooth and keep everything organized.
- **Tip:** Coordinate with all parties to be sure copies of the contract are distributed promptly, keeping everyone in the loop.

Pending Phase:
- **Contingency Negotiations:** Review credit and repair requests provided by the buyer. Be mindful in your delivery and come prepared with solutions to keep the deal together, if in the best interest of your seller.

- **Tips:** Keep your sellers focused on their "why" and help them take emotion out of the negotiation process.

Closing Preparation:
- **Smooth Closing Coordination:** Tackle the closing preparations with gusto, making sure every "i" is dotted and "t" is crossed as you head towards the finish line.
- **Tip:** Keep a checklist handy in your back office to track every task leading up to the big day, and remind sellers to cancel property services and transfer utilities.
- **Celebratory Closing:** Make the final walkthrough and closing a celebration. You want your sellers to feel pampered and praised for their trust in you.
- **Tip:** Gift your sellers a thoughtful closing gift to remember this successful partnership.

Post-Closing:
- **Continued Care:** Just because the deal is done doesn't mean your relationship is. Keep those lines of communication open to turn happy sellers into lifelong clients, even if they move out of your service area.
- **Tip:** Send a heartfelt thank-you note and invite them to share their feedback on their experience, perhaps over a cup of coffee.

By embracing this structured approach, you're not just processing transactions; you're creating lasting impressions that turn clients into fans. While many tasks can be automated to improve efficiency and allow you to focus on money-making activity, do not underestimate the power of communication. You should be communicating with your clients regularly—whether they prefer calls, text, or email. Remember, this is one of the biggest transactions of their life, if not the biggest. Commit to a weekly check-in with each client, even if there is no new news to share. They will appreciate hearing from you more than you know. While we may close dozens or even hundreds of transactions a year, they likely only do this every couple of years. If you support them through each phase with care, every client will feel like they're the star of the show, with their needs expertly managed and their expectations beautifully met.

MASTERING THE ART OF EFFICIENCY

Let's make every minute count! When it comes to managing your workload, it's all about working smarter, not harder. Let's roll up our sleeves and cut through the daily grind with some seriously smart strategies that'll transform how you tackle your to-do list.

- **Batching Similar Tasks:** Imagine handling all your emails in one swoop, scheduling client calls back-to-back, or dedicating a block of time just for your social media management. Batching similar tasks reduces the start-stop-start disruption that drains your energy and eats into your productivity. It's like meal prepping for your workweek: do it once, do it right, and enjoy the benefits for days.

- **Strategic Time Blocking:** Time blocking isn't just about marking appointments on your calendar; it's about consciously creating periods when you're laser-focused on specific activities. Allocate specific hours for client meetings, administrative work, and even brainstorming sessions for your marketing strategies. By guarding these time blocks fiercely, you ensure that every minute of your day serves a purpose.

- **Leveraging Technology:** Don't forget to let technology give you a helping hand. Automate where you can, from using your CRM to prompt you when it's time to reach out to a client to utilizing email and text automation. These tools act like your behind-the-scenes crew, keeping the show running smoothly so you can shine in the spotlight.

- **Prioritizing Tasks:** Not every item on your to-do list deserves the same urgency. Learn to prioritize tasks based on their impact and deadlines. Tackle high-priority items during your peak productivity times and save the lower-stakes stuff for when you're winding down.

- **Delegate:** Remember, being superhuman isn't necessary. Delegate tasks that don't require your personal touch to team members or outsource to trusted professionals. Whether it's handling paperwork, managing social media, or even administrative duties, freeing up your time means you can focus more on closing deals.

- **Regular Reviews:** Lastly, make time to review your processes regularly. What's working? What's not? Adjust and adapt. Streamlining isn't a one-time setup; it's an ongoing process of refining your methods so they continue to work best for you.

By incorporating these techniques, you'll notice that your days feel less scattered and more structured. You'll find more time for what truly moves the needle—and yes, that means more time for your clients and maybe a little extra for yourself. Here's to working efficiently, so your real estate business doesn't just grow; it thrives—while you maintain that precious work-life harmony. Ready to make every workday a little more brilliant? Let's do this!

> Today's preparation
> sets the stage
> for tomorrow's success.

9

Building a Support Network

Leveraging Relationships for Business Growth

Let's get real for a moment: the journey through real estate can often feel like a solo trek. Yet, the truth is, your path to success is richly paved with the relationships you build along the way. One key insight from my journey? It's crucial to cultivate a vibrant, supportive network of contacts. These aren't just acquaintances who exchange business cards with you; they're the cheerleaders, challengers, and collaborators who provide invaluable insights and open doors to new opportunities, enriching both your professional and personal life.

In this industry, perfection can be an illusion. Real estate is humbling, filled with endless learning curves. You'll never know everything—there are simply too many variables.

Acknowledging this has brought me peace, easing the pressure to always have all the answers. Instead, I focus on building strong connections. It's about knowing who to call when you need help, quickly turning to those trusted experts in your circle. This network isn't just about support; it embodies the spirit of President John F. Kennedy's famous saying, "A rising tide lifts all boats." Together, we grow stronger and reach higher.

THE POWER OF YOUR PROFESSIONAL CIRCLE

All right, let's dive into the heart of why your tribe—your network—is absolutely indispensable on your real estate journey. Picture your professional network as more than just contacts; they're your personal board of advisors, your cheerleaders, and sometimes, your much-needed reality check. Cultivating these relationships isn't just beneficial; it's transformative. But remember, this tribe isn't the same as the real estate dream team we assembled in Chapter 2. These folks are here to propel you forward, sharing and supporting your vision of success. They're invested in your wins and celebrate your victories as their own.

Nurturing this network transforms it into a powerhouse of mutual support and shared success. Let's explore how each connection within your tribe can push you to greater heights, ensuring you never walk your path alone, but alongside those who root for you every step of the way.

MENTORS WHO LIGHT THE WAY

Picture this: a go-to guru, someone who's already navigated the path you're treading, familiar with the good, the bad, and the ugly. In real estate, mentors are truly priceless, offering the kind of wisdom that only comes from years of hands-on experience. Whether you're wrestling with a complex negotiation or adjusting to an unpredictable market, a mentor can provide the pinpoint advice you need precisely when you need it most.

One of the most heartwarming aspects of my own brokerage is seeing our veteran agents—our OGs (original gangsters)—generously guiding our newer agents. It's not just about passing down knowledge; it's about fostering a culture of support and growth that lifts everyone.

PEERS WHO PROPEL YOU FORWARD

Let's dive into the world of your peers—those vibrant souls navigating the same real estate waters as you. These aren't just colleagues; they're in the trenches with you, the ones who truly understand the hustle. It's not about competition; it's about collaboration and mutual growth. They know the daily grind and the dedication required to excel.

Sharing triumphs and setbacks creates an environment of collective learning and resilience. Whether it's brainstorming over coffee or co-hosting open houses, each interaction is an opportunity to challenge and uplift each other. Your peers don't just enrich your professional life; they accelerate your growth, ensuring you reach new heights together.

When agents first join our brokerage, they undergo a training program that naturally forms cohorts among newcomers. This group becomes a mini-community within the larger brokerage, leaning on each other as they learn the software, navigate our processes, and settle into their new professional home. As we've seen, every brokerage operates a bit differently, and having a peer group to navigate these new waters can significantly enhance how well you adapt and thrive in your new setting. Let's harness the power of peer support to transform challenges into victories and create a thriving environment for everyone.

SUPPORT WHEN IT COUNTS

Let's face it—real estate can be a rollercoaster. Having a support network means you have people to lean on when things get tough. Whether it's a deal that falls through or a market downturn, your tribe can offer support, encouragement, and advice on how to pivot and persevere. A diverse network brings together varied perspectives that can enrich your professional life. These perspectives can challenge your own viewpoints, push you towards more innovative solutions, and help you see beyond what you thought was possible.

Your tribe is much more than a list of contacts—they are your support system, sounding board, and a critical component of your success. By investing in these relationships, you ensure that you're as well-rounded and informed as you can be, equipped not just to survive in the industry, but to thrive. Embrace the power of connection and make it a cornerstone of your real estate career!

CONNECT LIKE A PRO

Okay, let's talk networking—because it's about way more than just exchanging business cards and adding LinkedIn connections. It's about creating authentic relationships that are mutually beneficial and genuinely engaging. Whether you're shaking hands at a local chamber of commerce event, sharing a coffee at a BNI meeting, or chatting at a real estate conference, effective networking is your secret weapon in building a robust professional community. Here's how to make those connections feel natural and engaging.

Be a Giver, Not Just a Getter: This is your networking golden rule. Enter every networking opportunity with the mindset of "How can I help?" rather than "What can I gain?" For example, if you meet a new real estate agent who's struggling with digital marketing, offer to share your favorite tools or resources, or perhaps connect them with a marketing expert you trust. This approach not only sets a positive tone, but also makes you memorable.

Make Your Follow-Up Memorable: The real magic of networking happens in the follow-up. Don't just send a generic "Nice to meet you" email. Personalize it! Mention something specific from your conversation, like, "I loved hearing about your renovation project in downtown—such a cool venture!" Maybe attach a link to an article about a similar topic, or suggest a quick coffee chat to dive deeper into a discussion you started.

Keep the Connection Alive: Staying engaged is key. It's not just about reaching out when you need something. Make it a point to check in periodically with your contacts. Send them a note when you come across something that reminds you of them or if you find an event they might love. For instance, if you know someone loves modern architecture, send them an invite to a webinar featuring a renowned modern architect. Or if another contact mentioned enjoying a certain kind of cuisine, let them know when a new restaurant opens up in their area. These thoughtful touches keep relationships warm and show that you value the connection beyond a professional level.

Leverage Social Media Wisely: Use platforms like LinkedIn, Instagram, or Facebook to celebrate your connections' achievements publicly. Congratulate them on promotions, successful projects, or personal milestones. This not only strengthens your relationships, but also helps build a community where support and positivity are at the forefront.

By weaving these strategies into your networking efforts, you transform routine interactions into rich, lasting connections. It's about making every conversation count and every relationship a pathway to mutual growth and success.

HARNESSING THE POWER OF CONNECTIONS

Here's a little secret: your network is a goldmine of opportunities waiting to be tapped into, and learning how to gracefully leverage these connections can seriously catapult your career to new heights. It's all about mastering the art of the ask—a skill that can open doors, spark collaborations, and accelerate your growth.

Asking with Grace: When you need advice on a tough deal, feedback on your latest marketing endeavor, or a gentle nudge into the referral zone, knowing how to ask is crucial. It's not just about what you need; it's about how you make the other person feel when you ask. Approach each request with respect and clarity, ensuring that your contacts feel valued and appreciated, not just utilized for their expertise.

Creating a Two-Way Street: People are much more inclined to lend a hand when they see that the relationship is a give and take. Before you reach out with a request, think about how you can also offer value. Maybe it's offering to share their content with your network, providing a unique insight into the market, or even volunteering your time to support their causes. Make it clear that you're not just there to take, but also to give.

Timing is Everything: Just like in comedy, timing in networking is critical. Gauge the right moment to ask for help —preferably when your contact isn't overwhelmed with their own commitments. A well-timed request after a positive interaction or when they've just celebrated a success can lead to more enthusiastic assistance.

Be Specific: When you're asking for something, be as clear and concise as possible. Whether you're seeking advice, feedback, or a referral, lay out what you need, why you need it, and what you hope to achieve with it. This makes it easier for your contact to provide exactly the kind of help you're looking for.

By leveraging your network with these mindful strategies, you turn every interaction into a potential steppingstone for growth. Remember, your network is filled with people who are eager to support and lift you up in your journey. Let them be part of your success story, and don't forget to do the same for others. It's about growing together, expanding horizons, and turning individual achievements into collective triumphs. It's time to harness the power of connections and grow in ways you never thought possible!

NURTURING YOUR NETWORK WITH GRATITUDE

In the hustle of building a successful real estate career, it's easy to forget one of the most heartfelt principles of networking: gratitude. Celebrating and appreciating the support of your network isn't just a courtesy; it's a crucial part of nurturing and sustaining meaningful connections. Expressing gratitude can transform professional relationships and build a vibrant, supportive community around you.

Celebrate Their Wins: When someone in your network hits a milestone—whether they close a big deal, receive an award, or even celebrate a work anniversary—cheer them on! Drop them a congratulatory note, shout them out on social media, or even treat them to lunch. Celebrating their successes not only strengthens your relationships, but also creates an environment where everyone feels valued and supported.

Thank-You Notes: Never underestimate the power of a handwritten thank-you note. In a digital world, taking the time to write a personal message on paper can make a lasting impression. Send these out after meetings, when someone gives you advice, or when a colleague refers a client your way. It's a classic touch that shows deep appreciation for their time and effort.

Acknowledge Publicly: Whenever you get a chance, acknowledge the help you've received from your network in public forums. This could be during a team meeting, at a networking event, or through a LinkedIn endorsement. Public acknowledgment not only makes your contacts feel good, but also enhances their reputation alongside yours.

Gifts of Appreciation: Sometimes, words might not be enough to show how much you value someone's impact on your career. Consider sending small gifts as tokens of appreciation. This could be something as simple as a gift card to their favorite coffee shop, a book you believe they would enjoy, or even a custom gift that's relevant to a conversation you've had. It's a thoughtful way to show you care and pay attention to what matters to them.

Be There for Them: Finally, remember that appreciation is a two-way street. Show up for your network the way they have for you. Support their events, offer help when they're overwhelmed, and be a sounding board when they need advice. By being a reliable and supportive figure in their professional lives, you not only cultivate a culture of mutual respect, but also build lasting loyalty and friendship.

By integrating these practices of celebration and appreciation into your networking strategy, you create more than just connections—you build a community. This approach ensures that your network feels cherished and that their contributions to your success are recognized and celebrated. Make it your mission to not only achieve your goals, but to uplift those around you on their journeys too!

> Chase your dreams
> with heart
> and hustle.

Epilogue

Your Launchpad to Success

"So...I want to write a book," I blurted out to Nate, my husband, as we crossed paths in the hallway of our bedroom. Even though he's accustomed to my wild ideas, this one seemed to catch him by surprise. His immediate volley of who, what, and why questions soon gave way to words of encouragement, though I could tell he was processing the idea.

Truth be told, I'd been toying with the thought of writing a book for some time. Every time I meet a new agent or hear of someone eager to dive into real estate, there's so much I feel compelled to share to empower and guide them on their journey. While I'm confident in my knowledge, the thought of distilling it into a book was downright daunting. Okay, let's be real: *it was absolutely terrifying.*

But after a bit of an internal pep talk, I found the courage to finally voice this goal out loud. Speaking it into existence transformed it from an idea into a tangible goal. The more I talked about it, the more feasible it became to transfer those thoughts to paper. And now, here we are—you and I, at the end of this journey together.

Let's take a moment to soak this in. It might feel like we've hit the finish line, but truly, this is just the starting point. For you, it's the dawn of an exciting career in real estate. For me, it marks the beginning of my journey as an author—that's right, a bona fide author! In the spirit of Slim Shady, it's both "Crazy Insane and Insane Crazy."

In my years of leadership, I've realized that the lessons we share are often the ones we ourselves need the most. Every piece of advice, every strategy I've poured into these pages, mirrors my own journey in real estate. It's like having a heart-to-heart with my past self, acknowledging both the triumphs and the trials I've encountered along the way.

In this ever-evolving journey, we remain lifelong learners, absorbing lessons from the quietest days to the most chaotic, exhilarating moments. Everything around us—every client interaction, every closed deal, every missed opportunity—whispers valuable lessons. Trust me, even the subtle moments have profound wisdom to share.

Embarking on a career in real estate is much more than a professional choice; it's a deep dive into personal growth. It demands unfiltered honesty with yourself, a steadfast commitment to your values, and a relentless pursuit of excellence. This path isn't just about selling houses—it's about understanding and nurturing the person you meet in the mirror each morning. It requires patience, kindness towards yourself, and an immense amount of resilience.

So, as you turn these final pages, release the pressure to have all the answers right now. Cast aside any doubts that whisper *You're not ready*, or that the insights in this book aren't meant for you.

There are two gifts I hope to leave you with: the courage to ask tough questions and the strength to forge your own answers. Let this book be a testament to your capabilities and a reminder that you are, unequivocally, enough. Here's to not just chasing your dreams, but *living* them, vibrantly and fully. As we close this chapter together, remember: this is just the beginning of your adventure in real estate. Let's step forward with confidence and start crafting your successful career, one relationship, one sale, and one dream at a time!

This isn't just the end of a book; it's the beginning of your most exciting adventure yet. Think of this as your ultimate motivational pep talk, a gentle nudge to step boldly towards your dreams and craft a career that doesn't just satisfy, but truly delights and fulfills you. You've been equipped with tools, strategies, and insights—all the essentials to build a thriving real estate career. From mastering the art of connecting with clients to building a support network that lifts you higher, we've covered ground that's set to transform the way you navigate this bustling industry.

Now, it's your turn to take these lessons and carve a path that's uniquely yours. Embrace the challenges as opportunities to grow, see every interaction as a chance to learn, and never forget the "why" behind your hustle. Remember, the world of real estate isn't just about closing deals; it's about opening doors—to new possibilities, new homes, and new beginnings.

So, here's to you, the dreamer, the doer, the future shaper. Go out there, chase those dreams with all you've got, and build a career that lights up your heart. And always remember, you've got this—because the best agents aren't just made; they're self-crafted with grit, grace, and a whole lot of heart. Make your real estate journey one for the books, filled with success, satisfaction, and joy. Here's to moving forward, one successful transaction at a time. You're ready—and the world of real estate won't know what hit it!

XO
Jessica Souza

Acknowledgements

To my incredible husband, Nate:

How do I even begin to sum up our amazing journey together? From those sweet, young days when I was seventeen and wildly in love, through the twists and turns of military life, and every day after, you have been my rock. Each challenge we've faced has only deepened the love and admiration I hold for you. Being your wife is an honor that fills my life with joy.

From the moment I first saw you, my heart knew it had found its match. And with each passing year, our love uncovers new depths, continually surprising and delighting me. You've been my guide through some of my darkest days and loved me even when I felt unlovable. Your love is a gift I cherish deeply.

You're the first to encourage me to chase down my dreams, no matter how lofty or wild they may seem. Whether I'm dreaming up a new venture or diving into the unknown, you're there, my steadfast believer, fueling my confidence and quieting my doubts with your unwavering support and endless encouragement. Your faith in me gives me the courage to leap, your love gives me strength, and your partnership makes every adventure worth embarking on.

Jessica Souza

Thank you for being the solid ground beneath my feet, my cheerleader, and the love of my life. I am infinitely grateful for you and all that you do.

Here's to more laughter, dreams, and wild adventures together. Because if I know us—and I do—the excitement is just getting started!

I love you forever and always.

XO
Jess

Appendix I

Realtor ® Rearview

Step into the "Realtor® Rearview," where seasoned pros leave heartfelt notes to their rookie selves, sharing the wisdom they've gathered through the ups and downs of their real estate journeys. Each message offers advice they wish they'd had when they were just starting out. Whether it's tales of triumph or lessons from missteps, each shines with the kind of insider insight that can only come from years in the game. Perfect for agents seeking guidance, or anyone who loves a good "if I knew then what I know now" story, take a moment and connect with the collective wisdom of those who've already walked the road you're embarking on.

As a Realtor, it's essential to stay humble and honest, focusing on clients' needs. Don't make it about compensation. Save your money for your future, but prioritize great service that leads to referrals. By listening closely, enjoying the process, and continually growing, you'll build lasting trust and success.

—*Janet Shawen, Paradise Exclusive Real Estate*

If I could tell my younger self anything as a new agent, it would be to embrace trying new things in real estate—it will pay off. Don't wait for everything to be perfect; take action, be consistent, and learn as you go. Your authenticity is what will connect you with clients, and the relationships you build are more important than any sale. Trust yourself, stay curious, and remember, even in the toughest times, you're capable of thriving.

—*Sue Pinky Benson, Florida Realtor®*

You're sold on the logic behind the idea of focusing on sphere selling, but you're an introvert and only have a small group of close personal relationships that you won't want to introduce business into. That realization will create churn in growing your business. Think about this important decision now, play to your strengths and personality, and focus on your marketing while building a business sphere.

—*Jim Smoak, Former Agent and PropTech Product Management Professional*

I'd tell myself to be like a racehorse & keep my blinders on! The more we look around to see what others are doing while trying to reach the finish line, the slower we go. Once I figured this "blinders" trick out, my career hit the fast track!

—*Stacey Soleil, SVP Community & Engagement Inside Real Estate*

Don't think just because you can sell satellite dishes and hot tubs, you will be able to sell houses. Join a high-performing team and do a ton of deals. The experience and leadership you get, as well as the knowledge, will shortcut your road to success, and you will make so much more money faster. The amount you take home is more important than the high split. And last, all high performers have a coach—find someone who has been where you want to go and is willing to not buy into your bull crap so you can eliminate all of your excuses for failure. Remember, no other success can compensate for failure in the home, so don't stop paying attention to what matters most in search of the money.

—*Verl Workman, Workman Success Systems*

Always seek better ways to help others get what they want in life, and you will always be valuable. Make the experience worth sharing about, and your clients will always send you more opportunities.

—*Brad Nix, Path & Post Real Estate*

Relationships are crucial in real estate. Build and care for your network early and often! Find a mentor and a niche and become an expert in one area instead of trying to be everything to everyone. Most importantly, invest in real estate! (I'm glad I did that last one!)

—*Leslie Guiley, Real Estate Advisors*

Jessica Souza

Tim, invest in the skillset of teaching conversion. Tim, read more leadership books and learn from other leaders' mistakes, instead of making them on the fly in your business. Tim, set a standard for internal accountability, and stay consistent with it and enforce the consequences of poor actions without regret.

—*Tim Caudill, Florida Life Real Estate Group*

I feel like I took a good approach to being a newbie in real estate. However, I do feel that many don't take into consideration that they need to build long-term, sustainable relationships in this business. You might not think you'll be doing business with the same person very often, but you'd be surprised at how many times you will cross paths and how important that relationship is to making each transaction run a little smoother.

—*Brian Faro, Paradise Exclusive Real Estate*

One thing I've learned over the years is that being able to create your own schedule is a myth—you'll be working constantly to build your business and communicate with your clients, but the income potential is unlimited if you put in the work. Don't take it personally when friends and family don't use you—it's just business. Stay positive and keep networking. Know your market inside out, focus on customer service, stay consistent, and the clients will come!

—*Cali Rethwisch, Virtue Group at kwELITE*

Embrace every challenge as a stepping stone to growth, for each setback will teach you invaluable lessons. Build genuine relationships with clients and colleagues; they are the foundation of your success. Remember, patience and perseverance are your greatest allies in this journey —trust the process and keep pushing forward.

—Suzie Savage, Savage Real Estate Group
brokered by eXp

You are capable of more than you realize. Investing in yourself and your education will always be a decision you'll be proud of. Establishing clear boundaries, both in life and in business, is essential to your success. And remember, documentation always prevails over conversation—put it in writing.

—Ally Garcia, The Mooren Group
Paradise Exclusive Real Estate

Appendix II

Extras

Ready to take your real estate savvy to the next level with some fabulous freebies? You've turned the last page, but the journey doesn't end here. I've put together some exclusive extras just for you. Just a quick QR code scan away, and you'll unlock a treasure trove of resources designed to elevate your career sky-high.

So whip out your phone, give that code a scan, and let's dive even deeper. Because why settle for just what's in the book when there are so many more secrets to uncover? Here's to continuing our adventure and building the thriving career you've always imagined!

Suggested Further Reading

Each of these books enhances the lessons from *The Agent Playbook*, providing you with richer insights into mindset, sales techniques, and the real estate industry's finer points. Perfect for agents eager to elevate their careers and create lasting success!

***The Millionaire Real Estate Agent* by Gary Keller**—This guide is crucial for agents aiming to significantly boost their productivity and success in the real estate market.

***Mindset: The New Psychology of Success* by Carol S. Dweck**—Explore the influential concept of fixed vs. growth mindsets to enhance resilience and adaptability in your career.

***How to Win Friends and Influence People* by Dale Carnegie**—A timeless resource on improving interpersonal skills and building meaningful relationships, essential for real estate success.

***Sell with a Story: How to Capture Attention, Build Trust, and Close the Sale* by Paul Smith**—Learn the art of storytelling in sales, a valuable skill for standing out in the real estate field.

***Influence: The Psychology of Persuasion* by Robert Cialdini**—Master the art of persuasion to better understand and meet client needs effectively.

***Go-Givers Sell More* by Bob Burg and John David Mann**—This book expands on the idea that giving is the most fulfilling and effective path to success, a principle that can transform your real estate practice by focusing on value over profit.

***Shift: How Top Real Estate Agents Tackle Tough Times* by Gary Keller**—Perfect for navigating the unpredictable waves of the real estate market, this book offers strategies for thriving in any market condition.

***The Power of Habit: Why We Do What We Do in Life and Business* by Charles Duhigg**—Understand the science of habit formation to improve both personal efficiencies and client interactions.

***The Challenger Sale: Taking Control of the Customer Conversation* by Matthew Dixon and Brent Adamson**—A look into why challenging the norm and offering unique insights can lead to better sales results.

***Building a StoryBrand: Clarify Your Message So Customers Will Listen* by Donald Miller**—Learn how to effectively communicate your brand's message and make your real estate business stand out.

About the Author

JESSICA SOUZA is a licensed real estate Broker and Co-Owner of Paradise Exclusive Real Estate, a boutique brokerage in Southwest Florida. She has a passion for empowering agents and fostering their success. With years of experience in the field, Jessica is dedicated to transforming new agents into skilled professionals through insightful mentorship and innovative strategies.

If you discovered a typo while reading, please use the "Typo Correction Form" at the link below to report it and help maintain the accuracy of this book.

http://www.jessica-souza.com/book-typo

www.ingramcontent.com/pod-product-compliance
Lightning Source LLC
LaVergne TN
LVHW031735160125
801487LV00020B/57/J